LAW IN PRACTICE

Sally Lloyd-Bostock

A British Psychological Society Book
Series Editors: Professors A. J. Chapman and A. Gale

LAW IN PRACTICE

Applications of psychology to legal decision making and legal skills

Sally M.A. Lloyd-Bostock
Centre for Socio-Legal Studies
University of Oxford

LYCEUM
BOOKS, INC

224 S. Michigan Avenue
Chicago, Illinois 60604

AKP8951

First published in 1988 by The British psychological Society, St Andrews House, 48 Princess Road East, Leicester, LE1 7DR, in association with Routledge Ltd., 11 New Fetter Lane, London EC4P 4EE.

© Copyright Sally Lloyd-Bostock 1988
© Copyright Lyceum Books, Inc. 1989

All rights reserved. No part of this publication may be reproduced or transmitted, in any form or by any means, without permission.

Published in the United States by
LYCEUM BOOKS, INC.
224 S. Michigan Avenue
Chicago, Illinois 60604

Library of Congress Cataloging-in-Publication Data is available.

ISBN: 0-925065-06-4

Printed and bound in the United States by Malloy Lithographing, Inc., Ann Arbor, Michigan

Library of Congress Cataloging-in-Publication Data

Lloyd-Bostock, Sally M.
    Law in practice.

    "A British Psychological Society book."
    Includes bibliographical references.
    1. Psychology, Forensic. I. Title.
K5462.L59   1989   347'.07'019   89-14573
ISBN 0-925065-06-4   [342.77019]

To Kit and Alex

Acknowledgements

This book covers many specialist areas and I have relied extensively on others who work in the different areas to read and comment on bits of the book that fall within their expertise. I would especially like to thank Graham Davies, Gisli Gudjonsson, Lionel Haward, Keith Hawkins, Mavis Maclean, Mike Maguire, Judith Maxwell, Robert McHenry, David Mingay, William M. O'Barr, Ken Pease, Martin Richards, Avrom Sherr, Don Thomson, William Twining, and Neil Vidmar. Responsibility for what remains is of course mine.

The style of a book such as this has meant keeping references to people's published work to a bare minimum. There are good reasons for this, but it has meant drawing on many studies and ideas without giving the reference. I would like to thank all those whose work has contributed to the substance of this book, but whose names do not appear.

Lastly, my thanks to Jeanette Price for her painstaking and patient work on preparation of the manuscript, and to Peggy Lloyd-Bostock for her sketch of a biased line-up.

CONTENTS

Acknowledgements	vii
Foreword	xiii
Introduction	1

1. THE ACCURACY OF WITNESSES — 3
   - The honest witness — 3
   - The psychology of perception and memory — 5
     - Meaning and expectations • Memory for stressful events • 'Murder in the Corridor' • Forgetting
   - Aids to recall and recognition — 10
     - Identikit and Photofit • Identification parades • Other methods of establishing identity • Hypnosis
   - *In conclusion . . .* — 21

2. QUESTIONING SUSPECTS — 24
   - Techniques of interrogation — 24
     - The psychology of deciding to confess • Vulnerable suspects and confession reliability
   - Lie detection — 30
     - Validity of the polygraph • The polygraph and confession • Countermeasures to the polygraph
   - *In conclusion . . .* — 35

3. PERSUASION IN THE COURTROOM — 37
   - Credibility of the source of information — 37
     - Language style – powerful vs. powerless speech, narrative vs. fragmentary style, 'hypercorrect' testimony style, interruptions • Impact of eyewitness testimony
   - The message itself — 45
   - The medium — 46
   - Juries — 47
     - Juror characteristics • Systematic jury selection • The competence of jurors • Comprehension of instructions • Jury deliberations
   - *In conclusion . . .* — 59

4. SENTENCING ... 61
The sentencer's task ... 61
Sentencing as a cognitive skill • Why not ask the sentencers? • Sentencers' accounts • Pruning the decision tree • Biases • Expected patterns • Idiosyncrasies in sentencing • Feedback to sentencers

The sentencer in context ... 70
Factors related to sentences imposed • Gravity of the offence • Prior record • Characteristics of the sentencer • 'Framing' of the information received by sentencers • Psychiatric reports • Options and resources

In conclusion 80

5. CHILDREN AND THE LAW ... 83
Children as witnesses ... 84
Emotional effects of involvement in a court case • The reliability of child witnesses

Children and divorce ... 90
Initial reactions • Longer-term effects • Custody and access • Psychological theory • The effects of divorce vs. death of a parent • Divorce for the children's sake

Juvenile delinquency ... 99
The scale of the problem • Individual factors (sex differences, intelligence, other factors) • Family influences • Films and television • Responses to juvenile delinquency

In conclusion 105

6. COMMUNICATION SKILLS OUT OF COURT ... 108
Interviewing ... 109
Skilful client interviewing • Sources of difficulty • Physical surroundings • Opening the interview • Types of question • Pauses • Reflections and summaries • Other techniques • Clues to others' feelings • Other barriers to rapport • Giving advice • The interview as a whole

Negotiating ... 118
Tough or co-operative? • What makes negotiating strategies work? • The client's eye view of negotiation

Using clear language ... 127
Commonly used words vs. unusual words • Concrete vs. abstract words • Homonyms •

Synonyms • Negations and opposites • Long and complex sentences • Active vs. passive voice • Variety in style • Organization and layout of information
    From theory to practice 133

7. PSYCHOLOGISTS AS EXPERTS 137
    Types of psychologist 137
        Psychologist or psychiatrist?
    On what issues can psychologists act as experts? 141
    The methods used by psychologists as experts 145
        Clinical assessment and psychological testing • Special studies • More general advice
    How to find the right psychologist 151
    Psychologists' dilemmas in acting as experts 151
        Who is the client? • The ethics of taking sides • The pressure to give definite answers • Who presents the psychology to the court? • The use and misuse of psychologists in court • Being cross-examined
    In conclusion 156

8. A BROADER VIEW OF PSYCHOLOGY'S USEFULNESS 158
    The laboratory and the real world 158
    When can psychology be applied to real life? 160
        Making research realistic • The amount of research evidence • Theory • Are the findings significant? • Is it relevant to a practical problem?

AUTHOR INDEX 171
SUBJECT INDEX 175

Foreword

For the 700 or so years that lawyers have been trying cases, they have been asking themselves policy and strategy questions concerning those trials. They ask policy questions for the good of society: What rules of procedure and evidence will promote the just resolution of disputes? They ask strategy questions for the good of their clients and themselves: What strategies will make it most likely that our side will prevail? Indeed, what good trial lawyer has not, at some time or another, wondered about the answers to such questions as these:

- What are the conditions under which a witness will most accurately perceive, store, and retrieve information about an observed event? What are the factors that affect such memory? What effects do different approaches to eliciting such memories have on the contents of the memory and the recall? How can one test the accuracy of a witness' memory?
- How does one assess the fairness of a lineup, the accuracy of other police identification or interrogation procedures?
- What do average jurors believe about eyewitness accuracy? What credibility assessments do jurors make about different kinds of witnesses in different kinds of situations answering different kinds of questions — not only eyewitnesses, but also expert witnesses, children, parties to the case? What is it about witnesses and their testimony that most affects jurors' judgements? By what methods can these juror assumptions and assessments be modified?
- What is the process by which jurors reach their individual conclusions during a trial? What is the relative influence of opening arguments, the testimony of witnesses, closing arguments, and the deliberation process? How do the conclusions of individual jurors combine to produce a group verdict? What can a lawyer do to exert some influence on this decision-making process?

- What kinds of jurors are most favorable to one side of a case or the other? How important is the composition of the jury to the outcome of a case? How important compared with the evidence or arguments presented in the case?
- What determines the rulings a judge will make?
- Before the trial, what techniques of negotiation are most likely to bring about a favorable settlement?
- At trial, what are the most important determinants of the judge's or jury's verdict? What determines the amount of damages a jury will assess?

Fortunately, a tremendous overlap exists between the questions that lawyers ask themselves about trials and the empirical research that several different subfields of psychology have been doing for much of the past century. In recent years some psychologists have become active collaborators with attorneys and have pursued the answers to trial-relevant questions more deliberately. Other psychologists have pulled together the available knowledge into forms that lawyers will find easy to digest and use. These contributions to the lawyer's need for answers come from the research of experimental psychologists, who study perception and memory, cognitive psyichologists, who study decision making, and social psychologists, who study persuasion, negotiation, and group decision making, among other topics and subfields.

Little of this knowledge traditionally has been incorporated into legal education — although it is starting to appear in the curriculums of some law schools. And although some large law firms working on select large cases have obtained the help of behavioral scientists for trial preparation, this knowledge has not been readily available to most trial practitioners.

This book offers important and accessible help to legal practitioners who want to utilize the latest findings of empirical research on the trial process. Its author, Dr. Sally Lloyd-Bostock, is Britain's leading social psychologist interested in applications to the legal system, and she is well known to American research psychologists with similar interests. She is as conversant with research by Americans on the U.S. legal system as she is with British research on the British legal process. Her clear, plainly written book provides an excellent brief introduction to many of the questions that legal practitioners seek answers to; in addition, major reference works cited at the end of each chapter enable readers to dig deeper into a topic or to seek answers to still other questions.

Michael J. Saks
The University of Iowa

Introduction

Practising lawyers spend much of their time dealing with other people, whether they are interviewing clients, negotiating, preparing legal documents, or taking part in legal decisions and courtroom procedures. Research in psychology relates to all these aspects of law in practice. The psychology of communication, persuasion, and social interaction can help lawyers develop their legal skills. Psychological research on legal processes, both inside and outside the courtroom, can suggest ways of understanding what is going on from a psychological perspective: Why are eyewitness accounts often inaccurate? What makes a witness persuasive in court? How do judges and magistrates arrive at a sentencing decision? How do juries react to instructions?

In addition, psychologists are increasingly acting as experts in legal contexts. Most of the expert advice provided by psychologists relates to individual cases, involving psychological questions about such matters as the mental state of an accused person; or the likely effects of a custody decision on a child. Psychology has also been brought to bear on more general policy issues, for example through influencing judicial policy making or through advising Royal Commissions. Insights from psychology can shed light on practical legal problems and processes, without necessarily giving rise to specific advice in the individual case. The reliability of confessions, and the impact on children of testifying in abuse cases are examples.

A book on the applications of psychology to law in practice could range very widely indeed. I have simply not attempted to cover some areas. I omit psychology's contribution to substantive law, though psychologists have worked on policy questions about such matters as gambling and traffic law. Other topics can only be dealt with briefly: further reading is suggested throughout the book for those who wish to follow something up in more depth. I focus on the courtroom and the ordinary non-court work of most practising lawyers. I begin in Chapters 1 and 2 with questions about the reliability of witnesses and techniques of interviewing suspects. Chapters 3 and 4 then turn to the courtroom itself – the impact of evidence, language in court, juries and sentencing by judges and magistrates. The special issues raised by cases concerning children are discussed in Chapter 5. Chapter 6 moves right away from court work, and shows how principles of psychology can be applied to the skills of interviewing, negotiating and making legal language comprehensible. Chapter 7, on psychologists as experts, describes how different kinds of professional and applied psychologists apply their expertise in individual cases.

The research I draw on has been carried out in various parts of the world, including the UK, the US, Canada and Australia. It therefore comes from a range of different jurisdictions. As well as broader differences between, say, the UK and the US, law and procedures can differ between states in the US, or between England, Scotland and Northern Ireland. Few of these differences matter for the purposes of this book. Unless there is a specific reason to do otherwise, I shall simply refer generally to the UK, the US and Canada (or North America), or Australia. Occasionally Northern Ireland and Scotland need to be excluded from the UK and these instances are specified in the text.

I deal with some controversial topics. In some fields (such as the skills of interviewing clients) well-established psychological theory and research can be applied in a clear and direct way. But in others, psychologists feel that they are not yet ready to make sufficiently definite statements for legal purposes. Both lawyers and psychologists continually debate where the line should be drawn. Should the courts allow psychologists to provide expert evidence on the reliability of a witness's evidence? Can psychologists provide the right answers to questions about the best interests of children? When should the psychological 'knowledge' offered by psychologists be preferred to legal decision makers' own common sense?

There are good reasons to tread carefully. Most psychological research is not designed to answer practical questions. I have more to say in Chapter 8 about the question of when research findings can safely be put to practical use in legal contexts. In Chapter 7, I discuss some of the scientific and ethical dilemmas raised for psychologists who take on the role of expert. But I would not be writing this book if I did not believe that psychology has a great many interesting and useful things to say to practising lawyers, and perhaps to those interested in reform.

Chapter 1

The Accuracy of Witnesses

Witnesses are often extremely unreliable, not just because they may be lying. As Lord Devlin wrote in 1976, 'The highly reputable, absolutely sincere, perfectly coherent and apparently convincing witness may, as experience has quite often shown, be mistaken'. Even the self-incriminating statements of a suspect undergoing questioning quite frequently turn out to be false.

The accuracy of an honest co-operative witness and the detection of deception in a dishonest witness raise two rather different sets of questions. The problems of reliability that arise from psychological processes of memory and recall when a witness is not deliberately deceiving are discussed in the present chapter. In Chapter 2 I move on to the issues that arise when questioning someone suspected of a crime or, at least, of concealing the truth.

THE HONEST WITNESS

Lord Devlin was referring particularly to the problem of mistaken identity, and it is through celebrated cases of mistaken identity leading to wrongful conviction that the spotlight has come to be turned on the unreliability of eyewitnesses. A series of *causes célèbres* has brought this home in a dramatic way: James Hanratty who was hanged, Patrick Meehan, Luke Dougherty, Laszlo Virag, George Davis who were convicted and sent to prison, and George Ince and Peter Hain who were brought to trial – all primarily on the basis of identification evidence that was later discredited. But the same observation applies to accounts of events and memory for scenes as well as the identification of people. Nor is the problem confined to wrongful conviction. Mistakes and omissions in eyewitness accounts and identifications also create problems for the police and innocent suspects, and for civil cases concerned with compensation rather than conviction. One professor of law, William Twining, argues that both psychologists and lawyers interested in eyewitness identification have too readily focused attention on wrongful conviction resulting from mistaken identity. They have not really questioned whether this is the most frequent or important consequence of misidentification (Twining, 1983). Yet a suspect wrongly identified, brought into the police station, questioned and subjected to an identification parade may suffer greatly even if no prosecution is ever brought. Peter Hain was never convicted, but he surely suffered greatly from mistaken identification.

As long ago as the turn of the century criminologists and psychologists were staging experiments to test the reliability of witnesses and demonstrating that eyewitness accounts are often very inaccurate indeed. Our memories may serve us extremely well for the most part, but human memory was not designed for the benefit of the legal system. When a person is asked to describe events or identify someone after seeing them only briefly and possibly not having paid a lot of attention to them, he or she is being asked to do something that the memory is not adapted to do well.

To understand when and why eyewitnesses are likely to be unreliable it is necessary to break away from misleading ideas about how human memory works. Present-day psychology has developed ideas about the nature of memory that are fundamentally quite different from the kinds of model we would tend to use intuitively. We think of memory and perception as passive, copying processes, rather like a camera or tape recorder, or to be more modern, a video recorder. We expect tapes and recordings to deteriorate. Photographs may fade. But we would be very surprised if we put away a blurred photograph of a man with straight hair and when we later took it out found a clearly focused photograph of a man with curly hair. In the same way, we do not expect our memories to change apart from fading. We do not expect them to become clearer as time goes on, or to alter, and we expect them to be related to the original event in a very direct way.

Such passive models of memory have now given way to the idea that perception and memory are *active* and *constructive* processes. Perception does not produce a record but an interpretation. Nowadays there is emphasis on what the person contributes to the process of perception and memory – his or her expectations, past experiences, beliefs and prejudices, and what he or she is trying to do at the time.

THE PSYCHOLOGY OF PERCEPTION AND MEMORY

Only a fraction of the signals that reach us from the outside world can be registered by our senses and even fewer are converted into lasting memories. The process of perception is therefore of necessity highly selective. Attention is paid to the important or relevant, and much is ignored. Short cuts and rules of thumb are used. Because attention is selective, the attention-worthiness of an event can be of considerable importance in determining how well it is remembered. If someone knows in advance that they will be questioned about something afterwards they can provide far more complete and accurate information than someone who has not been forewarned. On the other hand, it is possible for a bystander to an event to be able to say very little about what went on right under his or her nose. The person may not be particularly dreamy or absent-minded – it is simply not possible to take everything in.

Meaning and expectations

As well as being selective, perception is also *constructive*, building a meaningful picture or sequence and filling gaps in information. We make sense of things, and come to perceive them in terms of the sense we have made of them. The general point that perception involves a contribution from the perceiver is illustrated by children's jokes based on an unlikely leap of recognition that a sketch is of, say, the 'south side of an elephant going north'. Quiz games sometimes show a photograph of a familiar object taken from an unusual angle and contestants struggle to identify the object. What these have in common is the absence of any clear hypothesis or expectation as to what the object is. It is not immediately obvious how the material is to be organized. Once given a clue (the answer to the riddle; more of the photograph) the perceiver is at once able to make sense of the information.

The part played by expectations in perception is strikingly illustrated in a tragic case described by Robert Sommer in 1959. Sommer acted as an expert witness in the trial. The incident occurred in Canada. A man mistook his friend for a deer whilst out hunting, and shot him dead. When the event was reconstructed, a Royal Canadian Mounted Police constable had no difficulty in identifying a man as a man in these circumstances, casting doubt on the likelihood that the hunter had genuinely taken his friend for a deer. What differed of course were the expectations of the constable and of the huntsman. On seeing something move, the huntsman, expecting to see a deer, did indeed 'see' a deer. An additional contributing factor was that the huntsman wore red – a colour that is more difficult to see late in the day.

In his book *The Reliability of Evidence* (1972) Arne Trankell provides a good example of the way in which gaps may be filled to make a meaningful sequence. A lawyer was crossing town in a taxi during the rush hour. Suddenly, the car in front of the taxi stopped and a door swung open. The lawyer saw an old man pushed out, or fall out, and lie in the road. The lawyer later discovered to his surprise that his observations had been quite mistaken. The old man had been a pedestrian who was knocked down, not a passenger in the car. The lawyer had seen an open door and the old man in the road, and his perceptual processes had done the rest. This kind of mistake is particularly likely to occur when something dramatic seems to be happening: we quickly form an idea of what it is on the basis of rather fragmented information.

Memory for stressful events

If an event is extremely stressful or shocking, the effect can be to interfere very seriously with our ability to remember anything much at all about it. Memory for what happened before the shocking occurrence can be affected, as well as memory for what followed. Sometimes if a person cannot remember what happened, memory may gradually return or be recovered under hypnosis. But sometimes people never remember. In these cases it is possible that the process of creating a lasting memory was interfered with to such an extent that there is no memory to retrieve.

At less extreme levels of stress, there has been debate amongst psychologists as to whether the memory of a witness to something like a crime will be enhanced or worsened by the strong emotions that he or she may experience. The reason for this debate is that emotional arousal can work both ways, depending on the level of arousal and on the complexity of the task to be performed. A moderate degree of arousal generally increases cognitive efficiency. But at high levels of arousal the reverse is true, and performance on complex cognitive tasks drops off quickly. This is why moderate exam nerves can be a positive help, but too much nervousness is counter-productive. Working in the other direction, there are reasons why memory for stressful events might be improved. The chance that people paid close attention is increased. They may even anticipate the need to be able to describe events later and make an effort to commit detail to memory. It has also been found that the more deeply information is thought about or puzzled over at the time it is presented, the more likely it is to be recalled later.

Psychologists cannot study experimentally the effects of extreme arousal – it would not be ethical to frighten or otherwise arouse people that much. But experience of actual events such as hold-ups suggests that the high level of arousal is such as to produce poor recollection afterwards. But retrograde effects of shock are apparent even at quite low levels. In one experimental study by Elizabeth Loftus and Terence Burns (1982) subjects were shown a film of a hold-up, and later their memory for details of it was tested. In the film the robber is chased from the bank into a parking lot where two young boys are playing. In one violent version of the film the robber runs towards a getaway car, then turns and fires a shot towards two men in pursuit. The shot hits one of the boys in the face, and he falls to the ground, bleeding and clutching his face. A second, non-violent version is identical up until just before the shooting. Then the film cuts to inside the bank where the bank manager is informing employees and customers what has happened, asking them to remain calm.

Those who saw the boy shot in the face had poorer memory for that part of the film before the shooting than those who saw the non-arousing version. Just before the shooting a large number 17 is visible on one of the boys' jerseys. Only 4 per cent of those who saw the violent version got this right, compared with 28 per cent of those who saw the non-violent version. On 14 out of 16 items where recall was compared, those who saw the violent film did worse. Although the violence was shocking, this was just a film of a fictitious crime. Witnessing a real crime is even more likely to produce shock and arousal levels that interfere with, rather than enhance, the processing of information.

'Murder in the Corridor'

Experiments involving staged events such as mock shootings have in fact produced rather strong reactions of shock and enabled the investigator to study the reliability of witness accounts in these circumstances. One such study is described in detail by Trankell. He calls it 'Murder in the Corridor'. A student acted aggressively during a lecture, interrupting with questions challenging the relevance of the lecture. The incident was built up until the lecturer asked the student to leave and accompanied him from the room into the corridor. Further argument was overheard by the audience through the open door to the corridor, and finally shots and a scream. The audience was thrown into a state of shock and panic. The follow-up investigation revealed that many witnesses had experienced physiological reactions such as shaking, dryness in the mouth, cold sweat, and difficulty with breathing. It indicated also that their capacity as witnesses was seriously impaired. There was considerable inaccuracy in the 29 witness accounts obtained immediately after the event. Out of 772 statements about the occurrence, only 495 were correct. The collection of data continued over a considerable period of time and included an interrogation held a week after the experiment. Many of the questions concerned time – when various stages in the drama were reached, and how long the final stage lasted. It proved almost impossible to reconstruct the course of events correctly from the answers obtained. In particular the interval between the start of the student's critical questions to the end of the episode was overrated by all the witnesses – but to different degrees. Approximately one third gave estimates that were 1.5 to 2.5 times too long. Another third gave estimates which were approximately three times too long, while the rest were up to eight times too long. The actual time was 1 minute 54 seconds. The mean estimate was 6.5 minutes, and the highest was 16 minutes. The overestimation of the time that dramatic events last is a very consistent finding in research of this kind.

More recent research by Elizabeth Loftus and her colleagues has examined another factor that is likely to be important in crimes involving a hold-up or hostage taking. Attention is liable to become narrowly focused on a weapon, for example, and little else is taken in. This phenomenon has been called 'weapon focus'. Using special equipment to record where people are looking, Loftus has confirmed that people do fix their gaze on a weapon and look correspondingly less at the gunman's face (Loftus *et al.*, 1987).

In summary, there are several forces at play when people are witnessing a dramatic criminal event that may affect their ability as witnesses. Time is very likely to be overestimated and the sequence of events may be confused. Gaps in scanty information may be erroneously filled, and whole chunks of the episode not remembered at all. Attention may be focused on a gun to the exclusion, say, of the gunman's face.

Forgetting

One might expect there to be rather little to say about the phase during which a memory is held in store, except that the memory fades over time. But it is here that some of the findings that seem strangest arise. Forgetting, it seems, is not a passive process of decay but, like perception, is selective and constructive. Similar factors operate to distort memory in systematic ways towards, for example, what we would like to have happened. With time, detail may not just disappear, but may become displaced or abridged, so that what is remembered is an amalgam of several incidents of a similar kind, or a logical rearrangement of details. The precise connection between elements of an event may become confused. It is not unheard of for a witness to identify a member of the police force as the villain – presumably because he or she is associated in the witness's mind with the crime. More insidiously, an innocent bystander may be identified as the criminal. In the shorter term there is mounting evidence for the malleability of memory, most notably from a series of studies by Elizabeth Loftus and her colleagues in Seattle. Their programme of research has shown how subsequent occurrences seem to interfere with memory of the original event, scene, or face. Of particular importance are experiments showing that leading questions or overheard accounts by others can alter the account a witness gives, without the witness being aware of the alteration. Apparently the original memory itself is altered or obscured. A good example is a very well-known study by Elizabeth Loftus and her colleague Judith Palmer. People were shown a film of cars in a collision and asked to estimate the speed of the cars. With different groups different words were used to ask about the speed of the cars. Some were asked how fast the cars were going when they 'smashed', others when they 'collided', and so on. The average estimate of speed varied depending on the word used. Estimates were highest for 'smashed', followed in order by 'collided', 'bumped', 'hit' and 'contacted'. What is more, in a follow-up a week later, subjects who had been asked about the cars' speed using the word 'smashed' were more likely than the others to say they had seen broken glass in the film. In fact there was no broken glass. The use of the word 'smashed' had somehow in their memory given the event features of a more violent collision.

Another experiment showed that memory for a face could be affected by overhearing others describe it as having particular features. People in this experiment were asked to make up a Photofit picture of someone they met. Some of the experimental subjects had overheard somebody else describe the man as curly haired – although in fact he had straight hair. These subjects then often gave their own Photofit version curly hair.

There is some disagreement about what underlies these phenomena. Does the original memory become transformed as Loftus believes, or does the 'original' memory remain, but become superseded by later versions which obscure but do not overwrite it? If the original is only obscured, the chance of recovering it may not be lost for ever. However, the phenomenon itself is not disputed – the description or account a witness provides can be altered to a quite remarkable degree. Luckily people are much more resistant to suggestion concerning the central features of an event than peripheral detail, especially after a real event rather than a simulation, or film or slide show. One important implication is that if a witness can be shown to be wrong about peripheral details, this need not cast doubt on his or her memory for the essential facts (see Yuille and Cutshall, 1986).

A very important finding is that showing photographs can be one of the ways memory is altered. So great care needs to be taken about showing an eyewitness photographs of possible suspects. People who have seen a photograph tend to pick out the person in the photograph in a later identification parade. This actually happened in the case of George Ince who was tried for murder in 1973. The husband and daughter of the victim, who had also been shot, had observed the murderer for some 20 minutes. Both were shown photographs of Ince before picking him out from an identification parade. Another risky procedure is encouraging hesitant people to guess. They tend to make more errors on a later test of accuracy. It seems that when people give answers to questions and make descriptions they incorporate these into their memory of the event or person. They may not later be able to separate the original from the subsequent additions. Wrong answers thus take on a life of their own in the witness's memory. In the Ince case, the daughter made a tentative identification at first on the basis of the photographs, but became progressively more confident in her identification over the following few weeks.

AIDS TO RECALL AND RECOGNITION

At the stage of activating and using memory various special techniques have been found useful: Identikit, Photofit, the use of police sketch artists, cued questioning methods, identification parades, photographs and hypnosis. Spontaneous descriptions and accounts from witnesses tend to be incomplete and vague. At the simplest level, their performance can be much improved by providing cues, such as naming different features that the witness is invited to describe. It is generally much easier to say whether you *recognize* something you are shown than to *recall* something and describe it. So methods that include an element of recognition – for example in the process of putting together a composite picture or looking at photographs – can extract information not otherwise accessible. Sometimes returning to the scene makes it possible to recall events that occurred there. But, of course, it is very important to be aware of the danger that any of these techniques can contaminate or bias the account a witness gives. At the same time, the relationship between confidence and accuracy breaks down, as we saw with the Ince case. A witness can become convinced that he or she remembers, even though he or she may have been uncertain at first. Each time a story is recalled and run over, or an identification repeated, the effect is increased. This is why by the time a witness appears in court, coherence and confidence may be very poor guides to accuracy.

A promising development is the 'cognitive interview'. Edward Geiselman and his team in the US are applying principles of cognitive psychology to develop a system of interviewing for use by the police that elicits as much accurate information as possible, while minimizing error. For example, the witness is encouraged to use ways of triggering memory such as mentally reinstating the physical and personal context of the event in question. Interviewers are taught to avoid switching topics, and instead to allow the witness to exhaust all he or she has to say on one topic before changing to another. The method is still being improved, but already shows impressive results. After only four hours of training, a group of high school students were able to obtain nearly twice as much accurate information from witnesses as were police of many years' experience (see Geiselman, 1984 for an initial report).

Identikit and Photofit

Graham Davies, at Aberdeen University, has summarized the various methods of eliciting information about faces, and research findings comparing their effectiveness (Davies, 1983). Identikit was introduced in the United States in 1959 and came to the UK two years later. The kit consists of 568 sheets on which are line drawings of features – chins, eyes, eyebrows, hair, lips and noses. These can be superimposed in a special frame to form a composite picture. The first composite is based on the witness's cued description. The witness can then suggest modifications to the completed face until he or she is satisfied. Extras such as wrinkles, moustaches and glasses can also be added. There is now a second version of Identikit based on photographs rather than line drawings. Photofit is basically very similar to Identikit but uses photographs of features printed on thin card. The cards are fitted together rather than superimposed and the resulting face can be embellished further with a wax pencil. Photofit was invented by Jacques Penry and has been in use since 1970.

Computerized versions of systems for constructing likenesses from descriptions are now becoming more widespread. The basic ideas remain the same, but the features can be stored on a computer, and the process of fitting them together and modifying them can all be done on a computer screen.

Information on how effective systems such as these are in actual police investigations is rather patchy. It is also difficult to interpret, because the composite may have been only one of several factors of importance in an investigation. Davies refers to only a handful of studies. One found a clear-up rate of 14 per cent in 123 cases in California where Identikit had been used. Another study quoted detectives as claiming it had played an important role in 5–10 per cent of cases. A 1977 survey on Photofit suggested that the typical police authority used Photofit in about 80 cases a year. Out of 728 cases followed up over two months, Photofit had 'greatly assisted' in 5 per cent. Of the 19 per cent cleared up, Photofit had assisted in 25 per cent. Where sketch artists are concerned, Davies states 'one can only note the yawning gap' in information about its effectiveness.

There is rather more information on how these techniques work in the laboratory. Although researchers are cautious about generalizing from these to 'real life', some interesting discoveries have been made. One might expect that a visual system such as Photofit would work better than a verbal description, but this does not seem to be the case. The reason seems to be that such visual systems are fairly crude. The range of features is limited and hairstyles may be out of date. Even with the subject there in front of the operator it can be difficult to produce a good likeness. A sketch artist has more flexibility, but needs to be very skilled. A remarkable example of the successful use of a sketch artist occurred in April 1985. A woman was subjected to a horrendous attack by David Fretwell, and left for dead in a field with her throat cut. Fretwell had also sexually assaulted and murdered a 20-year-old student. The woman survived her ordeal and provided the police with such an accurate description of her attacker that he was arrested a few days later. *The Times* printed a photograph of Fretwell next to the artist's impression based on the woman's recollection (see Figure 1.1.). The resemblance is extraordinarily close. Fretwell was, however, in some ways 'easy' to describe – he had a beard and moustache, receding hair, and wore glasses.

Techniques for recalling and conveying information about faces are more likely to be successful if they fit in with the ways in which we actually perceive and remember faces. For example, a piece-by-piece construction is less likely to work well if in fact we perceive faces as a whole and pay more attention to how the various features relate to each other rather than to their separate character. The sequence in which a

The Accuracy of Witnesses /13

Figure 1.1. Artist's impression and photograph of David Fretwell. From *The Times*, 27 April 1985. Reprinted by permission of The Press Association Ltd.

face is reconstructed is also likely to work better if it relates to differences in the attention usually paid to different parts of a face. Psychological research on how faces are perceived, remembered and recalled or recognized is quite extensive. Recognizing other people is very important so it is not surprising that the process is complicated and sophisticated. At least two quite separate elements are involved. The subjective feeling of *familiarity* elicited by the face of a friend seems to be separate from the process of *deciding* whether or not a face is that of the person we think it might be. Evidence for this comes from research on victims of brain damage: in very rare cases it is possible to lose the quite specific facility to experience a sense of familiarity in response to a known face – a condition known as *prosopagnosia*. It is, of course, far more often the second, decision-making element that is of concern in legal contexts, where the problems usually concern identification of someone not well known to the witness. As psychological research proceeds, the exploitation of Photofit and similar techniques will be guided by new knowledge of the natural process of face recognition.

Identification parades

The identification parade has attracted a great deal of attention from psychologists, especially since the Devlin Report in 1976. The purpose has been to help develop methods that maximize the effectiveness of the parade and also maximize its fairness. Fairness has been measured in two ways. First, a parade must be a reasonable size. Size is not as simple as it seems, since what counts is the number of plausible foils, or *effective size* (Malpass and Devine, 1983). The point is well illustrated in Figure 1.2. The effective size of this line-up is one! Secondly, psychologists use as a measure of bias the probability of the suspect being chosen by *anyone* given the witness's description of the offender.

Size and bias taken together are concerned with the extent to which the suspect sticks out as the obvious choice. Shepherd *et al.* (1982) quote the example of James Hanratty. Hanratty was picked from a parade on which he was the only one with dyed hair. The press had publicized this, and the witness subsequently agreed that the identification had been made on the basis that his hair stood out 'like a carrot in a bunch of bananas'. The ethnic origins of parade members could also mean the suspect stands out. So also could clothing, especially if the suspect wears clothes similar to those worn by the criminal when the witness saw him or her. A source of bias might also lie in the knowledge of other parade members, who may tend to look at the suspect, or not stand close.

Figure 1.2. A biased line-up.

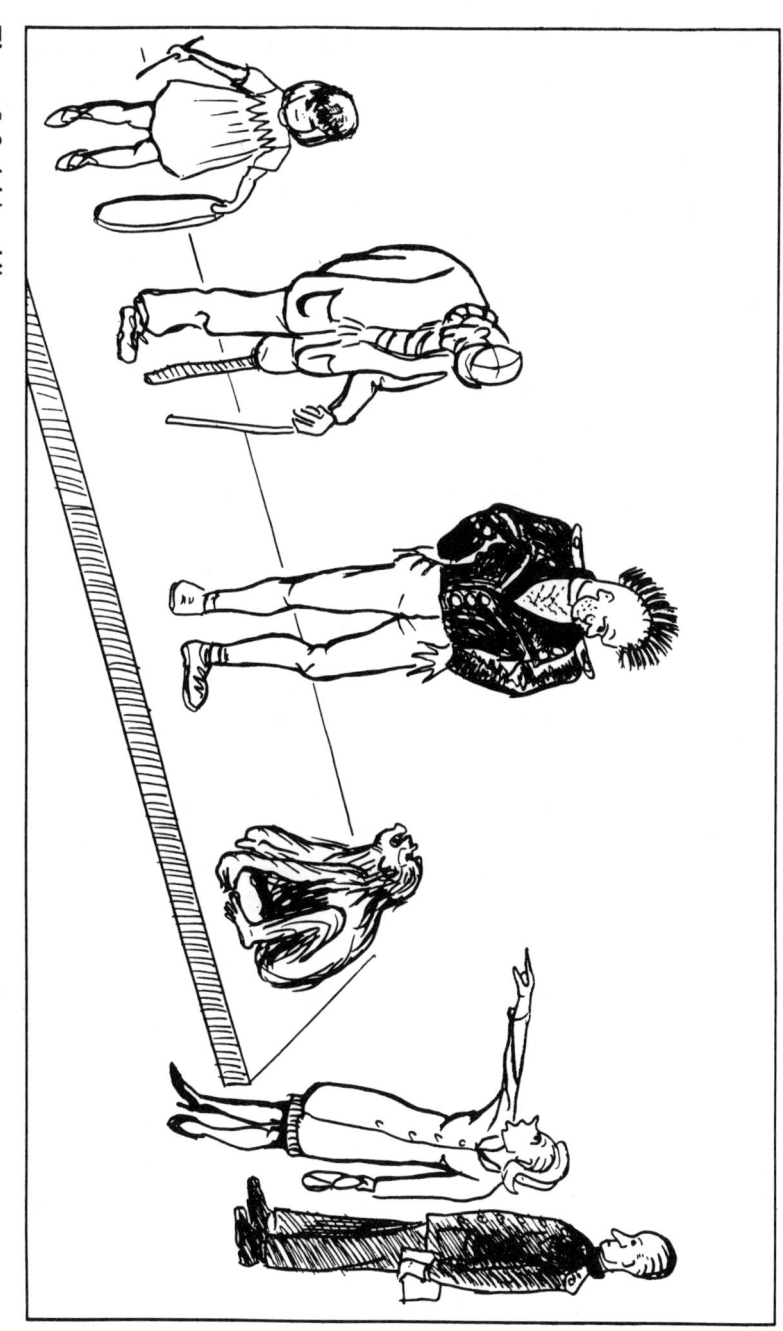

The instructions given to the witness can have a considerable influence on whether or not an identification is made at all. Studies of the effect of varying instructions in mock parades have shown that substantially more false identifications result if witnesses are influenced to make selection by biased instructions. In one study quoted by Shepherd *et al.*, when it was suggested to subjects that they should not necessarily pick someone, the rate of false identifications fell from 28 per cent to 4 per cent. What is more, Roy Malpass and Patricia Devine found that unbiased instructions (which did not imply that the subject should make an identification) reduced the number of false identifications without also reducing the number of correct identifications.

Not only explicit instructions define the task. There may well be more subtle social pressures to make an identification rather than reject the whole parade. The witness knows that the police have gone to a lot of trouble to put on a parade, and may also feel that the police must have their own reasons for suspicion. The whole process may also be rather unpleasant. Many people find it quite an ordeal, and as a result, may not make the best possible judgement.

Problems like these have led to empirical research on alternative methods of holding parades, including the use of one-way screens, but as yet, this research is not extensive, and the results are not clear cut. Some researchers (e.g. Dent and Stephenson, 1979) come out in favour of the use of photographs instead of a live parade; others (e.g. Hilgendorf and Irving, 1978) have concluded that the use of photographs is an inferior procedure, producing more false identifications. However, the use of some means of distancing the witness does seem helpful, and one-way screens have been introduced as standard practice in Scotland, South Africa, Denmark, Sweden and Washington DC for example.

Research on identification parades has tended to be framed as if their function is to produce reliable evidence for the courts. Parades may, of course, serve other functions, such as eliminating suspects from enquiries at an early stage, or persuading the culprit that the game is up and he or she might as well confess.

Other methods of establishing identity

Quite a range of identification procedures are used, including simply confronting the witness with the suspect, 'show-ups' and identification from photographs as well as various forms of the identification parade. A 'show-up' is a procedure whereby the witness is taken somewhere such as a pub, or the top of an escalator in an underground station, and asked to point out the person concerned if or when he or she shows up. From a psychological point of view this is a hazardous procedure. Since there is no control over who the other members of the public will be, there is no way of ensuring adequate foils. Having once made an identification at a show-up witnesses may then incorporate the identified suspect into their memory of the person they originally saw, so that other future identifications are influenced.

Hypnosis

The wonderful possibility of unlocking buried memories through hypnosis has, not surprisingly, led to considerable interest in forensic hypnosis. In the US hypnosis has been used by the Federal Bureau of Investigation (FBI) since 1968, as well as by other police personnel and crime investigators. Many psychologists are most unhappy about such developments. In particular, the practice of training policemen on a brief course to use hypnosis is condemned:

> That policemen who do not have a great deal of education in psychology should be encouraged to believe that they can become specialists in the retrieval of memory after a few lessons in hypnosis will strike many psychologists as ludicrous. That the results of their well-meant efforts can then be produced in court as 'evidence' strikes many of us as monstrous. (Gibson, 1982)

Lionel Haward (1981) also expresses reservations about the competence of police hypnotists to cope with the reactions of the hypnotic subject, especially where the protective device of shock amnesia is to be lifted. Considerable clinical and therapeutic skill may be needed to judge whether hypnosis is appropriate and to protect the mental health of the subject if it is carried out.

A large part of the problem of the reliability of accounts obtained under hypnosis lies again in the underlying theory of memory. Memory is all too often looked on as a kind of videotape. Indeed, some of the techniques of forensic hypnosis that have been taught explicitly use the idea of a tape that can be played back, rewound, frozen, and zoomed. The hypnotized subject is told to think of past events in this way, and asked to describe what he or she 'sees' on an imagined television screen as the imaginary tape is run, frames are frozen, and so on.

It is extremely dangerous for either hypnotist or subject to believe that this is the sort of process actually involved in memory. 'Exact copy' theories of memory are misleading. Memory is not laid down in this way and moreover the process of being questioned, recalling events, and so on, may interfere with it. This problem is a great deal worse when hypnosis is involved. People under hypnosis are in an extremely suggestible state, and are very open to any hints from the hypnotist as to what would be 'helpful'. A policeman who knows something about the crime, or who has strong suspicions about the villain, may cue the hypnotized witness, quite unintentionally, and create what Gibson calls 'pseudo-memories'. The hypnotized subject is later quite incapable of disentangling hypnotic fantasy from prior memories. Yet his or her confidence in the account given is likely to be strong. With or without hypnosis, going over a story or repeating identifications can transform an uncertain witness into a firmly convinced one. Hypnosis can serve to strengthen such effects.

A common technique is to use hypnosis to turn the clock back and regress the subject to the time of interest, bringing to the surface memories about that time. There have been claims that people can be taken right back to their childhood and remember in detail about, say, their class mates or a birthday party. Martin Orne, probably the most eminent expert in this area in the US, has cast serious doubt on the validity of these claims which, when examined closely, turn out to be based on questionable evidence (Orne, 1981). Orne has, for example, studied drawings done by adults regressed to childhood under hypnosis. He was able to obtain a collection of drawings actually done as a child by a man, now adult, whose doting parents had saved his every scrawl. This offered the fascinating possibility of comparing the drawings actually done by the child of six with drawings done by the same person, now an adult, but regressed to age six. When the man was regressed to age six and asked to do drawings while apparently 'back as a child' what he produced was totally unlike his actual drawings at that age. The drawings he produced were what an adult might think a child of six would produce; but they were not like those he produced when he was actually six years old.

In another example, Orne examined a study that seemed to show conclusively that memories not normally accessible could be brought out by hypnosis. The study involved taking subjects back in time to a childhood birthday. The subjects were asked questions about who came to their party and so on. The crucial question was 'What day is it?' This is something we would normally find impossible to recall – try and remember what day it was on your own eighth birthday! Yet the hypnotized and regressed subjects were able to answer remarkably accurately. It seemed their memories had indeed been reawakened and they were recalling events as if they were back on the day in question. The result puzzled Orne for some time, but he finally found the answer. The crux of the matter was the way in which the question had actually been asked. It turned out that the investigator had not simply asked 'What day is it today?', but had asked 'Is it Monday?, or is it Tuesday?. . .' naming all the days of the week. The investigator knew the correct day. The explanation of the result, Orne concluded, was that the investigator, quite unintentionally, was cueing subjects, through the intonation in his voice, as to which was the correct answer. The suggestible hypnotized subject obligingly then 'remembered' the correct day of the week.

What can hypnosis do?

Hypnosis is not then the wonder-tool that it has sometimes been held out to be. There is no video recording faithfully stored in the brain waiting to be uncovered and played back at the convenience of the forensic hypnotist: the appearance of clear and full recall under hypnosis can be totally spurious despite the best intentions of both witness and hypnotist. Why then do its users report examples of astonishing results where information obtained under hypnosis has been of great assistance in the investigation of crime? Before answering, let us consider two examples given by Lionel Haward (1981). In the first example, a man had spent the night wandering the streets. Circumstantial evidence pointed to him as the perpetrator of a serious criminal offence, and since he was unable to say exactly where he had been at the time the offence was committed, he was arrested. Under hypnosis he was able to recall passing some gas fitters checking a gas leak in a particular street, around midnight. The workmen had only been at the spot briefly, and this located him in place and time, excluding him as a suspect.

The second case concerned an apparent killing. A woman's body was found in a ditch. Tyre tracks over her body led to the suspect's car, and further evidence also pointed to him. He admitted taking her out for the evening, but he had got drunk and claimed he could remember nothing more. Under hypnosis, he recalled that they had both got drunk, and on the way home, he had pulled on to waste ground to allow the woman to urinate. She had got out, and he had passed into a drunken stupor. Many hours later he awoke, and finding the woman gone, had set off assuming she had gone home. It appeared however that she also had fallen into unconsciousness and slipped into a ditch. The accused had then unwittingly reversed over her when he set off for home. This account explained numerous otherwise inexplicable details, and was accepted by the jury in the case.

A number of possibilities may account for these and other examples of the positive usefulness of hypnosis. One is that under hypnosis the witness does indeed recall accurately details that he or she had not recalled before. Techniques such as imagining oneself back at the scene, and systematic questioning can, without an hypnotic trance, help the process of recall. These same factors may be operating during questioning sessions under hypnosis, and it is possible that the state of hypnosis may facilitate their operation further. Research into this possibility is currently under way by Geiselman in California, in conjunction with his work on the cognitive interview mentioned earlier. However, if this is the case, the problem of distinguishing fact from fantasy remains. Martin Orne, whose work on regressing hypnotic subjects was discussed earlier, concludes that neither the subject nor the expert observer can distinguish between confabulation and accurate recall in any particular instance. The only way this can be accomplished is on the basis of external corroborative data. Thus, it is certainly possible that hypnosis carried out by a suitably qualified expert may be of great help in some cases, but the dangers of the procedure and the limitations of its results must be fully appreciated if it is not to create far worse problems than it solves.

A second possibility is that a witness who has suffered a traumatic experience has shut out the memory. Under hypnosis, the relevant memories may be brought to the surface, along with the associated unpleasant emotions. There are several such cases reported (see, for example, Haward, 1981). But the same caution is necessary in using information obtained under hypnosis, or after hypnosis, where there is a condition of pathological amnesia as in any other circumstances. Some highly suspect 'recollections' may be reported.

However, the usefulness of hypnosis may sometimes be more apparent than real. The flow of information readily elicited under hypnosis may too uncritically be taken to be a flow of *accurate* information. A great wealth of apparently recalled material is often produced under hypnosis. Only when a controlled experimental study is made does it become apparent that the amount of factually correct information is no greater under hypnosis than without hypnosis. Gibson suggests that what may happen is that, as well as picking up cues from the hypnotist, people's own criteria as to what they accept as a true memory become relaxed under hypnosis, so that vague and incomplete recollections that would normally be rejected become constructed into memories and reported under hypnosis.

The conclusion to be drawn is that forensic hypnosis *must* be carried out by an expert, and its products used with extreme caution. The evidence of a witness who has undergone questioning under hypnosis should be looked on with serious suspicion. The use of hypnosis in legal contexts is not always to produce information about events. Orne, for example, successfully used hypnosis to explore and discredit the claim of the 'Hillside Strangler' to have a split personality. Properly controlled, hypnosis may be very useful in appropriate cases, but indiscriminate use and a false impression of its power can do a great deal of harm.

In conclusion . . .

Modern psychological theory and research have broken away from 'exact copy' theories of memory. Perception, memory and forgetting are now seen to be active, constructive processes. Information can be distorted and embellished in the process of perception. Whilst stored in memory, it can alter quite substantially and in ways other than just fading; the processes of questioning and recalling can further modify what is remembered. Techniques for eliciting information from eyewitnesses, such as cued questioning, use of photographs and identification parades must be designed to minimize the danger of interfering with memory and giving the witness misplaced confidence in his or her story. Hypnosis is especially risky, and evidence from witnesses who have been hypnotized is too unreliable to be admissible in court.

The practical advice that psychologists are able to offer about witness reliability can be much more definite on some matters than others. For example, quite precise statements can be made about the limitations on perception under particular lighting conditions. We know that the duration of events such as robbery is likely to be greatly overestimated. When the implications of existing research are uncertain, a special study can sometimes clarify matters in a particular case (see Chapter 7 for further examples of 'special' studies).

Often the implications for a particular case are uncertain, but implications for policy may be much clearer. For example, we know that showing photographs makes later identification parades unreliable. A psychologist will not be able to say that a particular witness will have been influenced by the photographs, only that a high proportion of witnesses would be and why. The risk is high enough that, as a matter of policy, safeguards are needed in police practice, and in the use made of the results of parades following the showing of photographs.

The advice psychologists can give depends also on the role permitted to psychologists by the law and legal professions. In the US psychologists have acted as expert witnesses in many cases involving the evaluation of eyewitness accounts. In the UK the evidence of psychologists as experts on eyewitness testimony has not been accepted, but psychologists have advised members of the legal profession on factors relevant to eyewitness reliability in a number of cases.

References

Davies, G. M. (1983) Forensic face recall: The role of visual and verbal information. In S.M.A. Lloyd-Bostock and B.R. Clifford (ed.) *Evaluating Witness Evidence: Recent Psychological Research and New Perspectives*. Chichester: Wiley.

Dent, H. R. and Stephenson, G.M. (1979) Identification evidence: Experimental investigation of factors affecting the reliability of juvenile and adult witnesses. In D.P. Farrington, K.O. Hawkins and S.M.A. Lloyd-Bostock (ed.) *Psychology, Law and Legal Processes*. London: Macmillan.

Devlin, Lord (1976) *Report to the Secretary of State for the Home Department of the Departmental Committee on Evidence of Identification in Criminal Cases* (The Devlin Report). London: HMSO.

Geiselman, R.E., Fisher, R.P., Firstenberg, I., Hutton, L.A., Sullivan, S., Avetissian, I. and Prosk, A. (1984) Enhancement of eyewitness memory: an emperical evaluation of the cognitive interview. *Journal of Police Science and Administration, 12*, 74–80.

Gibson, H.B. (1982) The use of hypnosis in police investigations. *Bulletin of The British Psychological Society, 35*, 138–142.

Haward, L.R.C. (1981) Expert opinion based on evidence from forensic hypnosis and lie-detection. In S.M.A. Lloyd-Bostock (ed.) *Psychology in Legal Contexts: Applications and Limitations*. London: Macmillan.

Hilgendorf, E.L. and Irving B.L. (1978) False positive identification. *Medicine, Science and the Law, 18*, 255–262.

Loftus, E.F. and Burns, T.E. (1982) Mental shock can produce retrograde amnesia. *Memory and Cognition, 10*, 318–323.

Loftus, E.F. and Palmer, J.C. (1974) Reconstruction of automobile destruction: An example of the interaction between language and memory. *Journal of Verbal Learning and Verbal Behaviour, 13*, 585–589.

Loftus, E.F., Loftus, G.R. and Messo, J. (1987) Some facts about 'weapon focus'. *Law and Human Behaviour, 11*, 55–62.

Malpass, R.S. and Devine, P.G. (1983) Measuring the fairness of eyewitness identification lineups. In S.M.A. Lloyd-Bostock and B.R. Clifford (ed.) *Evaluating Witness Evidence: Recent Psychological Research and New Perspectives*. Chichester: Wiley.

Orne, M.T. (1981) The use and misuse of hypnosis in court. In M. Tonry and N. Morris (ed.) *Crime and Justice: An Annual Review of Research, Vol. 3*. Chicago: University of Chicago Press.

Shepherd, J.W., Ellis, H.D. and Davies, G.M. (1982) *Identification Evidence: A Psychological Evaluation*. Aberdeen: Aberdeen University Press.

Sommer, R. (1959) The new look on the witness stand. *Canadian Psychologist, 8*, 94–99.

Trankell, A. (1972) *The Reliability of Evidence: Methods for Analyzing and Assessing Witness Statements*. Stockholm: Beckmans.

Twining, W.L. (1983) Identification and misidentification in legal processes: Redefining the problem. In S.M.A. Lloyd-Bostock and B.R. Clifford (ed.) *Evaluating Witness Evidence*. Chichester: Wiley.

Yuille, J.C. and Cutshall, J.L. (1986) A case study of eyewitness memory of a crime. *Journal of Applied Psychology, 71, 2*, 291–301.

Further reading

Lloyd-Bostock, S.M.A. and Clifford, B.R. (ed) (1983) *Evaluating Witness Evidence: Recent Psychological Research and New Perspectives*. Chichester: Wiley.

Loftus, E.F. (1979) *Eyewitness Testimony*. Cambridge, Massachusetts: Harvard University Press.

Wells, G.L. (1988) *Eyewitness Identification: A System Handbook*. Carswell Legal Publications, Toronto.

Chapter 2

Questioning Suspects

TECHNIQUES OF INTERROGATION

Considerable effort has been directed at developing techniques of police questioning of suspects. American police science manuals written by experienced interrogators contain detailed advice on strategy and practice. The most notable example was the 1967 edition of Inbau and Reid (superseded by a third edition in 1986). A central aim of these techniques is to elicit confessions. There may be several reasons why a particular suspect is being questioned in a particular manner, but usually the police are hoping to persuade the suspect that the game is up and he or she might as well plead guilty. Confessions rarely become evidence in court. A guilty plea almost invariably follows, and inquiries into the procedure that resulted in the plea of guilty are unlikely.

The use of 'psychological' techniques such as those advocated by Fred Inbau and John Reid has been highly controversial. On the one hand, the rights of the person being interrogated must be protected and the possibility of false confessions (or other false statements) minimized. On the other hand, a guilty person being questioned by the police would seem unlikely to volunteer a confession or information unless doing so is made an attractive proposition – or not doing so an unattractive one. In the US extensive debate followed the Supreme Court decision in the case of *Miranda* v. *Arizona* in 1966, which established the famous 'Miranda warnings'. (A person in custody must, amongst other things, be warned that he or she has the right to remain silent, and to an attorney, though these rights may be waived.) In the case of *Miranda*, the Fifth Amendment, which states that a person has the right not to be compelled to give self-incriminating evidence, was applied to questioning in police custody. In discussing whether the police interrogation practices amounted to compulsion, the court explicitly referred to manuals such as Inbau and Reid's. The picture of police interrogation that emerges from such manuals is somewhat dramatic and is unlikely to be representative of most routine interviews. None the less, police in the US are trained in and use the techniques they describe.

In the UK there has been less emphasis on training the police in interrogation methods, but a study by Barrie Irving in the Brighton Criminal Investigation Department (CID) confirmed that a very similar repertoire of techniques was used (Irving, 1980). The study is being repeated to see how the implementation of the Police and Criminal Evidence Act (1984), which came into effect in 1986, is affecting practice. As in the US, police interrogation is a controversial topic in the United Kingdom. In particular the Confait case in 1976 attracted a great deal of attention giving rise to an inquiry (Fisher, 1977). The suspect Lattimore, a young man of subnormal intelligence, falsely confessed to the murder of Maxwell Confait, and was convicted. The case highlighted the special problems of questioning the mentally handicapped, and has given rise to a programme of research in the area. Other cases are also causing concern. Questions are being raised about the reliability of the confessions of the 'Guildford Four', convicted in 1974 for their alleged part in the IRA bombing of a Guildford pub, now serving prison sentences.

Are current interrogation techniques successful?

There is no doubt that some of the techniques of interrogation that have been developed are highly successful in eliciting confessions and information that the suspect does not offer willingly, and with few exceptions the techniques are based on sound psychology. It has been estimated that seven out of ten interrogations result in a confession. Barrie Irving found that, of 60 suspects who were observed being interviewed, 35 made admissions during the interview. A further four made later admissions. Only 13 of the suspects actually resisted attempts to persuade them to admit, and five of these had an acceptable alternative account to offer.

It is possible that the effectiveness of interrogation in obtaining co-operation and confessions could be increased by further refinements of technique and by further training. However, it seems inevitable that a hard core of suspects (especially experienced criminals) will resist any attempts to persuade them to confess. The more serious problem can be that questioning techniques work only *too* well. There are powerful social and psychological forces at work in the whole experience of being in custody, suspected of a crime, and questioned by the police, which, if skilfully handled, can lead to confession, false or true. Confessions and statements made by accused persons ranked second only to mistaken identification as a cause of wrongful conviction amongst cases referred to the Court of Appeal by the Home Secretary, or in which free pardons were granted, between 1950 and 1970 (Brandon and Davies, 1973).

A comprehensive discussion of the kinds of technique advocated and used by police in the US and UK is given by Barrie Irving and Linden Hilgendorf, in evidence they prepared for the Royal Commission on Criminal Procedure in 1980. Their report is in two parts, the first relating Inbau and Reid's practical suggestions to the psychological literature, and the second relating both of these to actual practice as observed in the CID at Brighton. (The study of course predates the Police and Criminal Evidence Act, 1984, which introduced several changes in the rules surrounding police interrogation and the admissibility of confessions in court in England and Wales. At the time I write, a repeat of the study under the new system is in progress. It is already clear that major changes have taken place in the police interview room.)

The psychology of deciding to confess

Irving and Hilgendorf organize the very wide range of factors involved in terms of the costs and benefits of deciding to confess. Interviewing techniques can then be seen as working to alter or influence the suspect's view of the consequences of confessing or not confessing. They divide these into the utilitarian consequences, the social consequences, and consequences for the suspect's self-esteem.

Manipulation of the *utilitarian* consequences might, for example, include downgrading the seriousness of the crime or the likely sentence for such crimes. During his Brighton study, Irving observed remarks by interviewers stressing, for example, that if the suspect was honest and made a clean breast of it this would increase the likelihood of lenient treatment in court.

Examples of *social* consequences relate to the need for the approval of others who have a significant relationship with the suspect. If the interrogator skilfully builds up a relationship with the suspect then the interrogator's own approval can become significant. Examples observed by Irving include the interviewer emphasizing that being honest and confessing is the mark of a 'sensible' person, an 'adult' or an 'intelligent, reasonable' person. The officer expressed sympathy, understanding or empathy with the suspect's behaviour, thus playing down the negative social consequences that might follow conviction.

Thirdly, Hilgendorf and Irving discuss *self-esteem*. Suspects may refuse to admit an offence because they cannot accept a view of themselves as having committed that offence, or they may have a negative image of people who admit things to the police. Examples in the Brighton study of attempts to alter the way a suspect views himself or herself included emphasizing the suspect's good sense or likeable nature; pointing out how much better it would feel to get things off one's chest; emphasizing that the victim would think positively of the suspect for admitting the offence. Another way in which the police may affect the suspect's perception of the advantages and disadvantages of confessing is by giving the impression that there is really no decision to be made, and that, because of other evidence, the suspect will inevitably be charged and probably convicted. The 'other evidence' may often be simply bluff, and the police are well aware that this technique must be used with great care if it is not to misfire.

For the interviewing officer to exercise influence over the suspect's perceptions of his or her situation, it is necessary to establish and maintain authority. Manuals such as Inbau and Reid's emphasize this strongly and it is consistent with the implications of psychological research. The police are in a position to control the information available to the suspect, and to provide expert information on, for example, the likely response of a court. In addition, many of the consequences of confession may lie more directly in police hands. They may be in a position to exercise discretion over charge, bail and whether or not further lines of investigation will be pursued, and thus in a position to bargain.

The importance of the authority of the police does not lie solely in these comparatively straightforward powers to control information or to bargain. The relationship between an individual and someone in authority contains the potential for quite dramatic psychological effects. Stanley Milgram (1974) in a famous series of experiments illustrated the astonishing degree to which ordinary people would obey the instructions of an experimenter who had established a position of authority. Subjects in his experiments were willing to administer to other people what they believed to be extremely painful and dangerous electric shocks. Suspects being interrogated can become similarly over-acquiescent to the demands of an interviewer who has carefully established and maintained status and control over the situation.

Although the techniques in manuals on police interrogation are in general extremely effective, Hilgendorf and Irving point out some ways in which they are out of line with some psychological thinking. For example, Inbau and Reid describe a point of growing conflict in interrogation which indicates that a suspect is coming close to the point of deciding to confess. At this point the suspect is likely to fidget and dither and show confusion. They advocate keeping up the pressure at this point. However, pressure at this time is likely to be counter-productive. Indeed at another point in their manual they describe a more promising approach to dealing with decision conflict, which is to lead the subject away from the ultimate choice and thus take the pressure off, so that the suspect is not faced with making the critical choice until the right moment in the interrogation.

Hilgendorf and Irving also point out that Inbau and Reid are working with a dual notion of the causality of confessions and therefore are sometimes somewhat inconsistent in their advice. On the one hand they see confession as resulting from the suspect coming to believe that confessing is the reasonable course of action but, on the other, they also sometimes view confession more in terms of 'cracking' the suspect. But overt threats, a build-up of stress and pressure, and displays of force tend to be counter-productive as means of extracting a confession. There is a danger that the suspect will become over-aroused and this can produce a boomerang effect. When people (or animals) become very frightened, they respond by retreating or attacking. Similarly, an over-aroused suspect may withdraw co-operation in panic, or aggressively defy the interrogator. Some people in Milgram's experiments became extremely aroused and defied the experimenter.

As well as the authority of the interviewer, and perhaps the suspect's desire for the interviewer's approval, the suspect's decision may be affected by a whole set of situational factors to do with being in police custody. There is likely to be some degree of stress and anxiety associated with the whole process of being confined. Hilgendorf and Irving argue that factors in the situation such as confinement, social isolation, threat of harm and interrogation after sleep loss, perhaps at night, may all impair the decision-making powers of the suspect, leading to confession in spite of its negative consequences. However they concluded that in practice these situational factors were of secondary importance when compared with the mental state of the particular suspect.

Vulnerable suspects and confession reliability

Perhaps the most worrying finding from Irving's generally optimistic Brighton CID study was that nearly half of the suspects interviewed could be described as being in an abnormal mental state. Included in that group were not only those with some identifiable mental abnormality such as subnormality or mental illness, but also a substantial group who showed visible symptoms of fear. A further group were suffering from the effects of intoxication or drug withdrawal. In these conditions an innocent suspect may well be suggestible or unable to make a rational decision. But the researchers conclude that for any given suspect it can be virtually impossible to judge whether or not his or her mental state constitutes sufficient grounds for excluding the statements made on the basis of 'involuntariness' or 'oppression' which, at the time of the study, were the criteria for deciding the admissibility of a confession as evidence in court. The Police and Criminal Evidence Act (1984) has since abandoned 'involuntariness' and introduced a new criterion: the confession's 'reliability'. It is hard to see how this is any more workable. The change moves the focus of attention away from events in the police station towards an evaluation of the resulting confession, and thus possibly reduces the control by the courts of police questioning procedures. A confession could still be admitted as evidence even when police procedures in obtaining it are subject to criticism.

Questioning techniques and aspects of being in custody can certainly facilitate true confessions in the ways I have outlined, and hence perhaps legitimately expedite criminal process, but they may also lead to unreliable confessions and statements. Apart from some obvious outer bounds protecting the rights of the suspect, it is probably impossible to set out practicable limits on interrogation techniques that will overcome the danger of eliciting false confessions from suggestible and vulnerable suspects. At present it is not possible to do much more than point out the inherent dangers in *any* interrogation technique.

Work is currently under way on the particular problems raised by questioning people with mental handicaps. In addition to the problems of their mental handicaps, this group may present the added problem that they have been taught to present an outward appearance of confidence and normality. This seems to have happened in the Maxwell Confait case, where Lattimore appears to have learnt to avoid exposing his mental limitations. The Police and Criminal Evidence Act (1984) safeguards seek to protect some of the groups that seem most vulnerable – the mentally ill and handicapped, and drug abusers. Other work includes that by Gisli Gudjonsson, who is exploring the possibility of assessing individual suspects' susceptibility to techniques of persuasion to confess under police interrogation, and hence the reliability of statements they have made (Gudjonsson, 1984).

The question of the suggestibility of suspects overlaps with the question of the suggestibility of witnesses who are not suspects, discussed in the previous chapter. A similar debate is under way amongst psychologists as to whether a suspect's original memory for what happened is sometimes actually altered when he or she succumbs to suggestion, or whether the effect is to obscure rather than change the original memory, leaving the possibility that the original may still be recoverable. Further possibilities lie in the analysis of recordings of interviews which might reveal signs that a statement is untrue. More research on actual interrogation is needed for such tools to be developed.

LIE DETECTION

Techniques of lie detection depend on the uncomfortable emotions that for most people accompany the knowledge that they are lying. Sometimes this discomfort or anxiety may be manifested in readily observable ways such as difficulty in looking the other person in the eye or fidgeting. Gaze and facial expression are often relatively easily controlled by the liar and more helpful cues may be found in the hands or feet. The anxiety felt at lying though not shown in the face 'leaks out' in a tossing foot. But simply observing non-verbal behaviour of this kind at best provides only a clue that the individual may be experiencing anxiety or stress, the reason for which *may* be that he or she is lying.

A much more accurate indication of stress (which again may or may not be due to lying) can be obtained by taking physiological measures such as heart rate and blood pressure, sweating and rate of breathing. Increases in these characteristically accompany stress, and all can be monitored. This is the basis of the traditional polygraph 'lie detector'. The individual is wired up to the machine, which has pens which draw continuous graphs of electrodermal activity (indicating even very slight sweating as the conductivity of the skin alters), and respiratory and cardiovascular measures. The operator then questions the subject and examines the graphs made during the questioning session for indications of stress in response to particular questions.

The polygraph in personnel screening and other commercial settings now supports a thriving and dubious industry in the US. It is estimated that at least two million American citizens are confronted by a lie detection test every year, the majority in the process of simply applying for a job. Employers routinely screen applicants for 'honesty', as if this were a general and measurable personality trait.

It is important to stress that the polygraph does not detect lies as such:

it detects physiological responses characteristic of stress. It is up to the polygraph examiner to interpret the results. In the past claims have sometimes been made that a specific lie response has been found that uniquely identifies lies. This is not true. It is important also to note that the results of polygraph tests on some groups of people may be misleading – for example, psychopaths, the exhausted, those suffering from certain illnesses or people who are very distressed.

Since the polygraph does not detect lies, lie detection techniques concentrate on designing a series of questions that make signs of stress as unambiguous as possible. The tests must minimize the possibility that a result can be explained simply by the fact that the subject is just generally nervous about the tests or about any question concerning the incident (say a theft) that gave rise to the test, or about any questions concerning his or her honesty in general.

Polygraph methods

Various methods have been developed which compare responses to significant questions with responses to other questions. The main techniques are described in detail by David Lykken in his book, *A Tremor in the Blood (1981)* and, more recently in Anthony Gale's book *The Polygraph Test: Lies, Truth and Science* (1988). The methods all depend on the level of stress indicated by the polygraph being affected by the content of different questions. The techniques are of two fundamentally different types. David Lykken, who is an acknowledged expert in this field in the United States, refers to them as 'lie detection' and 'guilty knowledge' techniques.

Lie detection techniques include any where the goal is to distinguish lies from truth in answers to relevant questions. The form of questioning involves asking the subject directly relevant questions ('Did you steal the money?') and comparing the response with other neutral questions ('Is it Tuesday?'), or emotive but not directly relevant questions ('Have you ever stolen from a previous employer?'), or questions about a fictitious crime ('Did you do x?', when x did not occur). Interestingly, it does not make all that much difference whether the subject actually lies or not and on some tests he or she is told simply to answer 'No' to every question or even just to listen to the questions. The question itself elicits a physiological response. Lykken is highly critical of many current practices in the US, including the most widely-used polygraph method.

The *guilty knowledge technique* relies on there being certain facts that only the guilty person will know. The polygraph of a guilty person is therefore likely to show a reaction of stress at the mention of the true facts as compared with a fictitious alternative version of the facts. In his book Lykken engagingly illustrates the technique in the form of a fictional detective story, 'The Body on the Stairs'. This story retells a murder case in which only the murderer or someone else present at the murder would know details such as the position of the body, items on the floor, and so on. A guilty knowledge test could therefore be constructed in which the suspects were shown, for example, photographs of the body in various poses, and various different items on the floor. In each case only one item was taken from the true facts, the rest were plausible alternatives invented by the test constructor. Guilty knowledge was indicated by a consistently marked reaction to items giving the true facts as compared with alternative items plausible to someone not acquainted with the facts.

The technique has definite advantages and is discussed at length by Lykken. It is also described by Gudjonsson (1983) who has himself used it in practice. However, its use is rare, and polygraph examiners are not usually trained in the technique. The drawback is that the test requires there to be suitable 'guilty knowledge' available to the police but not to any innocent suspect. Publicity must be tightly controlled, and the police must be willing to take the risk of revealing critical information to suspects through the test. Also, the test should, if possible, cover several pieces of guilty knowledge so as to minimize the risk that the suspect is reacting to an item for some quite different reason, or conversely to maximize the chances of obtaining a clear pattern indicative of guilt. Moreover, a guilty person may not have a clear memory of the details of the crime especially if he or she was drunk at the time. For all these reasons the test is often just not practicable.

Validity of the polygraph

So just how accurate is the lie detector? Unfortunately the polygraph has some over-exuberant supporters who have in the past made rather exaggerated claims. Even discounting these, the evidence is far from clear. Evaluation of the validity of the polygraph is complicated by the fact that there are so many different techniques and applications (such as personnel screening). Also, in studies of actual uses of the polygraph (as opposed to laboratory studies) it is difficult to establish what is the truth, against which the findings of the polygraph can be assessed. In many applications, the polygraph itself is only part of the information the examiner uses. Much higher success is claimed for examinations that make use of the tester's clinical impressions as well as the polygraph test tracings.

Moreover it is necessary to balance the likelihood of mistakenly identifying an innocent person as a liar against mistakenly identifying a liar as truthful. A test which tends to be biased against the innocent may be less desirable than one with a higher error rate overall, but which is not biased against the innocent. It is therefore relevant to know whether when a test does result in misclassification, it tends to misclassify the guilty or the innocent. For example, Lykken discusses one study of the results of a lie control test on a sample of 56 criminal suspects, half of whom were guilty and half innocent. His 10 polygraphers in fact scored 63 per cent of the clients as deceptive, showing a bias against the innocent subject. Most of the actually guilty subjects (77 per cent of them) were correctly classified as deceptive, but only 51 per cent of the innocent subjects were correctly classified as truthful. In other words nearly half the innocent suspects were misclassified as deceptive. From the innocent suspects' point of view the polygraphers might as well have flipped a coin.

These kinds of results notwithstanding, those taking lie detector tests as a rule place great faith in the ability of the test to distinguish truth from lies. Indeed for some techniques to work it is important that subjects should believe in the power of the polygraph, and tricks may be used to establish this. For example, Lykken describes how, before taking the test, the subject may be asked to select a card from a pack of trick cards made up of, say, only Queens of Hearts. The polygrapher then demonstrates to the subject that by looking at the subject's polygraph tracing he can tell whether he or she is answering truthfully to such questions as, 'Is it a red suit?', 'Is it a face card?', until the polygrapher arrives at the answer.

The polygraph and confession

The faith the subject has in the test may account for the fact that its most useful aspect is not actually in detecting lies at all, but rather its extraordinary capacity for obtaining confessions. The faith of the subject is graphically illustrated by a celebrated case in Cincinnatti where an employee was being tested in connection with the theft of a few hundred dollars. The polygrapher was employing a technique which supplements the question and answer session with further probing questions, suggesting that the subject is showing a damning reaction to some of the questions. The technique often elicits a confession. In this case, in accordance with the technique, the polygrapher left the subject on his own to stew for a few minutes and observed him through a one-way screen. The subject was clearly agitated and finally tore off the six feet of paper on which the test tracings were recorded and proceeded to eat the lot! When the examiner returned he made no comment on what he had seen but began to prepare the next test. Then suddenly he leant down to the machine and said, 'What's that, he ate them?' This was too much for the respondent who said, 'My God, you mean it can talk!' and went on to confess to taking the money.

The case of Peter Reilly in Connecticut illustrates rather more tragically the dangerous degree of faith the police sometimes in the past had in the polygraph, as well as the astonishing degree of faith of a suspect. An account of the case is given in Bartlett's *A Death in Canaan* and is summarized by Lykken (1981). Peter Reilly, aged 18, came home one night to find his mother dying after a brutal attack. The police, summoned by Reilly, put him in a squad car to wait alone for three hours then took him to the state police barracks. He had a brief sleep and was then given a lie detection test. Hardly surprisingly he showed strong reactions to questions like, 'Last night, did you hurt your mother?' This was sufficient to convince the police that he was lying. The whole interrogation, including the lie detection test, was tape-recorded. The transcripts show how the police insisted that, because of what the polygraph charts revealed, Peter must have killed his mother; and how Peter himself eventually became convinced that he must have committed the crime even though he had no recollection of it. He believed he must somehow have shut out the memory. Peter Reilly signed a confession to the murder of his mother and it was two years before the confession was shown to be false. Lykken comments on this episode:

> Reading the transcript of the Peter Reilly interrogation, any sensible person should be able to recognise at once that this confession was meaningless, an eruption from seeds planted one by one in the mind of an exhausted and impressionable boy. The police, eager to 'solve' their case and blinded by a perverse and groundless faith in the polygraph apparently were satisfied they had their killer. (Lykken, 1981)

Countermeasures to the polygraph

Deliberate attempts can be made to beat the machine. There are two kinds of technique: attempting to suppress reactions to the critical items in the test, and deliberately producing physiological reactions to the control questions. The subject may try to control his or her responses by mental effort or by some physical trick such as tensing muscles or biting the tongue. Gudjonsson (1983) describes the various techniques in more detail and concludes that it is possible to affect the polygraph recording, but that the tests are more resistant to countermeasures if several physiological measures are taken simultaneously and if the examiner is alert to obvious attempts to distort the charts.

In conclusion . . .

The use of 'psychological' interrogation techniques and the polygraph are both controversial. Questioning methods that are effective in eliciting confessions from the guilty may also elicit false statements from the innocent. Psychological research on obedience to authority, conformity, persuasion and suggestibility has demonstrated the extraordinary power of quite subtle social and psychological dynamics in a situation such as being a suspect in police custody. Inexperienced criminals, people with mental handicaps and such like may be particularly suggestible and vulnerable.

Evidence in the US has shown that the polygraph also carries the risk of inducing people to confess falsely. In addition, the polygraph's validity is uncertain. Some widely used methods are open to serious criticism. The polygraph's 'benefits' lie more in its success at persuading people to admit the truth because they believe the test is infallible than in the test's actual power to discriminate truth from falsehood. In some cases the polygraph has proved useful to the police and to suspects keen to demonstrate their innocence. Errors can be minimized by proper training and by the use of the best and most appropriate technique. But it is evident that the booming polygraph industry in the United States has led to tragic mistakes and to abuse; and some of the exaggerated claims made for it are enough to make any self-respecting psychologist's hair stand on end. A working party of The British Psychological Society in 1986 expressed strong reservations about current uses of the polygraph in the US and concluded that some practices are contrary to the Society's Code of Conduct – such as giving subjects a false impression of the test's accuracy and inducing anxiety in them to encourage them to confess.

References

Brandon, R. and Davies, C. (1973) *Wrongful Imprisonment*. London: George Allen & Unwin.

Fisher, Sir H. (1977) *Report of an Inquiry by the Hon. Sir Henry Fisher into the Circumstances Leading to the Trial of Three Persons on Charges Arising out of the*

Death of Maxwell Confait and The Fire at 27 Dogget Road, London SE6. London: HMSO.

*Gale, A. (ed.) (1988) *The Polygraph Test: Truth, Lies and Science*. London: Sage Publications/ The British Psychological Society.

Gudjonsson, G.H. (1983) Lie detection: Techniques and countermeasures. In S.M.A. Lloyd-Bostock and B.R. Clifford (ed.). *Evaluating Witness Evidence: Recent Psychological Research and New Perspectives*. Chichester: Wiley.

Gudjonsson, G.H. (1984) A new scale of interrogative suggestibility. *Personality and Individual Differences 5*, 303–314.

Inbau, F.E. and Reid, J.E. (1967) *Criminal Interrogations and Confessions*, 2nd edn. Baltimore: Williams & Wilkins. (The third, 1986 edition, has three authors, F.E. Inbau, J.E. Reid and J.P. Buckley.)

Irving, B.L. (1980) *A case study of current practice*. Research Study Number 2, Royal Commission on Criminal Procedure. London: HMSO.

*Irving, B.L. and Hilgendorf, E.L. (1980) *Police Interrogation: The Psychological Approach*, Research Study Number 1, Royal Commission on Criminal Procedure. London: HMSO.

*Lykken, D.T. (1981) *A Tremor in the Blood: Uses and Abuses of the Lie Detector*. New York: McGraw Hill.

Milgram, S. (1974) *Obedience to Authority: an Experimental View*. New York: Harper & Row.

Further reading

Publications marked with an asterisk (*) above.

Chapter 3

Persuasion in the Courtroom

A barrister or solicitor presenting a case in court will usually be attempting to persuade a judge, magistrate and/or jury, of a particular argument or version of events, or perhaps of the appropriateness of a particular sentence. The processes of persuasion, attitude change, impression management, and social influence have been studied by social psychologists.

The factors governing how persuasive a communication is are often divided into three groups: those associated with the *source* of the message, the *message* itself, and the *medium* whereby the message is passed. A further set of factors relate to the *audience* that receives the message. I discuss each of these in turn, concentrating on research carried out with the courtroom in mind; but I draw out also some of the central findings from research in other contexts. As always, the application to courtroom settings of research carried out in other contexts must be speculative.

CREDIBILITY OF THE SOURCE OF INFORMATION

There are, of course, several sources of information in court, including a witness, a solicitor or barrister, and documents as well as face-to-face encounters. Psychological research in other contexts has found that sources of information are more persuasive if they are seen as possessing expertise and objectivity. If someone advocates a position against his or her own interests, that is particularly persuasive. Perceived power, status and prestige also enhance the persuasion. A message may be better attended to if the source is familiar, similar to the audience in attitudes or background, likeable, or physically attractive. Research specifically concerned with courtrooms is rather sparse but what there is has confirmed this general pattern.

Language style

An intriguing series of studies by William O'Barr (an anthropologist) and his colleagues Allan Lind (a psychologist) and John Conley (a lawyer) has shown that certain speech styles carry greater credibility than others. The studies (summarized in O'Barr, 1982) are part of the Duke University Law and Language Project based at Duke in North Carolina, and looked specifically at speech in the courtroom. Their research is especially interesting because they worked in two stages. First through observation of what actually occurs in courts, they discovered various different speech styles being used. Then on this basis, they developed an experimental stage to test the effects of these styles. In particular, the style the researchers identify as 'powerful' leads to the witness or advocate being seen as competent, trustworthy, dynamic, attractive – and convincing. I describe these studies at some length since they are both fascinating and directly relevant to courtroom practice.

The research team set out to look for the scientific basis, if any, for the extensive advice that exists on courtroom strategy. A great many quite specific techniques and strategies are recommended in various trial manuals, but these recommendations are based entirely on experience. How or if they work is not really considered. The authors of such manuals are experienced lawyers and their experience is their primary credential for offering very specific advice. The assumptions they make about how language and communication work are not made explicit, let alone tested.

O'Barr's research group identified four specific contrasting styles of speech that occur frequently in the courtroom: 1. powerful (versus powerless) speech; 2. narrative (versus fragmented) testimony; 3. 'hypercorrect' speech; and 4. simultaneous speech. They tape-recorded actual trials over 10 weeks to discover and analyse these styles. On the basis of the tape-recordings, they then prepared research tapes to use in their experiments. Actual stretches of testimony were selected, but the originals were modified to produce variations in style. Thus, a stretch of 'powerless' testimony was transcribed and rewritten to create a 'powerful' way of saying the same thing; and so on for the other speech styles. Both the original and the doctored versions were then recorded on tape. For each set of contrasting styles, one of the two versions occurred in court. The research differs in this respect from studies that are guided by theory and lack this basis in ethnographic work.

What then, are the features of these styles, and how do they affect the impact that testimony has?

1. Powerful versus powerless speech. The idea that there might be such a thing as 'powerful' speech and 'powerless' speech came from previous work suggesting differences in speech style between men and women. As well as research showing that male and female witnesses tend to speak in different styles, trial manuals often recommend special techniques for examining or cross-examining women. The main features of 'women's' speech identified by previous research were:

- Use of 'hedges', such as 'It seems like...', 'I guess...' rather than a straight statement;
- 'Super-polite' forms such as 'I'd really appreciate it if';
- Tag questions, such as 'John's here isn't he?' instead of 'Is John here?';
- Emphasis in intonation, like speaking in italics, using *so*, *very*, and so on;
- Empty adjectives, such as 'lovely', 'sweet';
- 'Hypercorrect' grammar and pronunciation;
- Lack of sense of humour;
- Use of direct quotation rather than paraphrase;
- Special words used only by women – such as 'magenta', 'chartreuse';
- Question intonation in declarative contexts, for example in response to the question 'When will dinner be ready?' the reply 'Around six?', as though this were a question asking whether that time is convenient.

The research team found that women did tend to speak in this style in court, but to varying degrees, and that men's speech also sometimes had many of these characteristics. They therefore analysed the effects of these characteristics in the speech of both men and women. They made tapes of powerful and powerless versions of basically the same stretch of about 10 minutes of questioning. Thus the answer 'Well we were, uh, very close friends. Oh she was even sort of like a mother to me' could be rewritten in a more 'powerful' form as 'We were close friends. She was like a mother to me'. In the 'powerful' versions, such features as hedges, intensifiers, hesitations, use of the term 'sir', were greatly reduced or omitted, but the factual information remained the same. It was found that at the extremes, speech styles for men and women did not overlap. It simply was not within usual bounds that a woman would speak in such a powerful style, or, even more unusual, a man in such a powerless style. Therefore two versions were made of the powerful tapes and two of the powerless tapes, one recorded by a male and one by a female actor.

The four tapes (powerful man; powerless man; powerful woman; and powerless woman) were played to experimental subjects, who then rated the witness on several dimensions. The results are summarized in Table 3.1. Statistical tests showed that all the differences between men and women were greater than might occur by chance. It is clear that witnesses speaking in a 'powerful' style are rated as more convincing and truthful than those using a 'powerless' style, even though the factual content of the testimony is identical.

2. Narrative versus fragmentary style. A similar procedure was used to investigate the effects of a narrative style, where the witness is allowed to give a long and full reply, as compared with a more fragmentary style, where the questioning is more detailed and the answers kept short and not elaborated. Although this difference is to some extent under the control of the questioner (see Chapter 6), O'Barr also found that witnesses tend to respond in one or the other style. The effect on the listener of either of these styles therefore was expected to be a combination of impressions of the witness, and of the questioner, and of the relationship between them. It might also be expected that a lawyer on

Table 3.1. Average rating of witness using powerful and powerless language.

	Female witness		Male witness	
	Powerful	Powerless	Powerful	Powerless
Convincingness	3.00	1.65	3.52	2.09
Truthfulness	3.70	1.88	4.24	2.86
Competence	2.61	0.85	2.44	0.18
Intelligence	2.57	0.23	1.80	0.18
Trustworthiness	3.04	1.65	3.48	2.00

From W.M. O'Barr (1982) *Linguistic Evidence: Language, Power and Strategy in the Courtroom.* Academic Press. Reprinted by permission.

direct examination would have more confidence in the witness and would therefore provide the opportunity for him or her to use a more narrative style, whereas a lawyer cross-examining a hostile witness might be expected to go for tighter control. The experiments used questioning on direct examination only and avoided this added complication.

The results were complex. Listeners' ratings of confidence in the witness depended on whether the witness was male or female and whether the person doing the rating had any legal training. Broadly however, the results showed a more favourable evaluation of witnesses giving testimony in a narrative style, and also a higher rating for what they believed was the lawyer's impression of the witness's competence.

3. 'Hypercorrect' testimony style. The term 'hypercorrect' is used to mean misapplication of the rules of grammar, or incorrect use of vocabulary, or inappropriate over-formality, in an attempt to speak in a style that is more formal than that which the speaker is accustomed to using. For example, silent letters may be pronounced; or a word or phrase such as 'during that interim', 'cognisant' or 'notify' used rather than 'in that time' 'aware' or 'tell'. 'Hypercorrect' speech is usually more precisely enunciated than is normal for that person, and therefore sounds 'overcorrect'. Witnesses in court quite often adopt a 'hypercorrect' style. The researchers hypothesized that witnesses using this style would be less favourably evaluated, because such a style would be associated with lower social status or the desire to ingratiate themselves with those listening to them. This hypothesis was confirmed. In an experiment comparing the two styles, the witness speaking in a 'hypercorrect' style was rated as less convincing, less competent, less qualified and less intelligent than the witness using a formal style without these 'hypercorrect' features.

4. Interruptions. Verbal clashes between a witness and a lawyer typically occur during cross-examination when the two vie for control over the presentation of testimony. These clashes are marked by interruptions of one by the other, and periods when both talk at once. Since who dominates whom could make a difference to how the interchange is perceived, O'Barr's team created four tapes. The experiment used a male witness. In one control version, there was no overlapping or interruption. In a second, neither lawyer nor witness dominated. In a third, the lawyer dominated, persevering in three quarters of the overlaps until the witness gave way, and in a fourth the witness dominated.

The results showed that the lawyer's control over the testimony was perceived as low in *all* situations where speech overlap occurred. It did not matter who dominated. Conversely, the witness was perceived as more powerful and more in control – whether or not the witness dominated in these exchanges. There were, however, some differences found between 'lawyer dominates' and 'witness dominates' situations. When the witness dominated, raters felt that he had more opportunity to testify and the lawyer was rated as fairer to the witness. In summary, the most favourably rated situation was that with no interruptions or overlap. When these did occur, the situation where the witness dominated led to more positive evaluations of the lawyer and of the witness's opportunity to present his or her version of the facts. By implication, a strategy of limiting verbal conflict by overpowering a witness would seem to be a dangerous one.

These studies of courtroom language are in many respects only a beginning and the interpretation of the results is often speculative. In addition, the 'subject jurors' used were students – their responses may differ from those of actual jurors containing a more mixed bunch of people. But the studies do have implications for understanding what is going on in verbal interchanges in court, and the likely impression different speech styles will have. Practical applications of this work have already shown promise – I return to this at the end of the chapter.

Before discussing the findings of his own research programme, O'Barr reviews and comments on the recommendations made in several trial manuals. It is interesting to look at some of these recommendations in the light of the research I have just been discussing. For example, O'Barr[1] lists as illustration some of the speech characteristics said in trial manuals to be associated with witness impact:

1. Overly talkative witnesses are not persuasive.

2. Narrative answers are more persuasive than fragmented ones.

3. Exaggeration weakens a witness's testimony.

4. Angry, antagonistic witnesses are less convincing.

5. Overly dramatic witnesses may come across as phonies.

6. Extreme slowness in responses is not convincing.

7. Too many qualifications of an answer are not good.

---

[1] From: W.M. O'Barr (1982) *Linguistic Evidence: Language, Power and Strategy in the Courtroom*. Academic Press. Reprinted by permission.

8. Using unfamiliar words to make an impression may be seen instead as insincerity.

9. New, original, or personal descriptions and analogies are more convincing than conventional, hackneyed ones.

Advice on lawyers' own verbal behaviour includes the following:

1. Personalize your own witnesses; distance yourself from an opposition witness.

2. Use variations in question format (extensive advice on the kinds of question to ask is offered in all the manuals).

3. Maintain tight control over witnesses during cross-examination: allow more opportunity to your witness for narrative versions.

4. Convey a sense of organization in your presentation.

5. Adopt different styles of questioning with different kinds of witnesses – such as men and women, the elderly, children, expert witnesses.

6. Remain poker-faced – save dramatic reactions for special occasions.

7. Rhythm and pace are important.

8. Repetition is useful for emphasis but should be used with caution.

9. Avoid interrupting the witness.

These examples of the kind of advice contained in trial practice manuals provide an interesting comparison with the findings that have emerged from the empirical studies carried out by O'Barr and his colleagues. Advice in trial manuals frequently has an ambiguity about it – it is qualified with riders that it may work for some occasions and not others, and manuals often suggest discretion in the use of techniques and strategies. None the less, there is some interesting overlap in the general aspects of speech style found relevant to credibility. O'Barr's studies suggest how these speech styles have their effect.

Impact of eyewitness testimony

One area that has received special attention amongst psychologists has been the impact of eyewitness testimony. This interest arises as one side of a much wider interest in questions about the reliability of witness evidence (see Chapter 1). An important reason for this wider concern has been the great impact that eyewitness testimony seems to have. Research (with mock jurors) has demonstrated that eyewitness evidence is highly persuasive, and is given too much weight, a phenomenon that has been called the 'overcredulousness' of jurors. In one set of studies, eyewitnesses were believed 80 per cent of the time, regardless of their actual accuracy.

However, they are not always believed. The question is, when is inaccuracy suspected? A clear finding is that people rely on the confidence of the witness. This is perhaps not surprising. But research has frequently shown that confidence is not always a good guide to accuracy. The relationship between confidence and accuracy varies considerably. There is, initially, a high correspondence between feeling sure of a memory and being right – but this correspondence can be destroyed when something occurs to alter confidence, or to alter accuracy, but not both.

For example, we saw in Chapter 1 that experiences such as questioning after an event can alter and distort the way in which the event is recalled. But studies have shown that these same experiences may well not alter confidence. Indeed, confidence in a memory may *increase* as a result of repeating a story over and over again in response to questions, or discovering that a particular account is regarded as likely by others. Confidence may be increased while accuracy is unchanged or reduced. For instance, the form in which questioning is carried out can involve the witness in making a positive commitment to an account. 'Don't know' answers may be discouraged and guessing encouraged. The process of questioning can increase confidence by reinforcing replies, and conveying the expectation that a witness will know the answer.

As well as self-ratings of confidence, some studies have looked directly at the effects of the *appearance* of confidence. Priming witnesses prior to giving evidence in court can greatly increase their appearance of confidence, and with it their credibility.

The power of eyewitness evidence is such that research has shown it to have an effect on deliberations and verdicts even after it has been discredited. For example, in one simulation study the witness was revealed to be so short-sighted that the evidence was totally discredited, yet verdicts showed an effect of the testimony that was almost as great as when it was not discredited. Another study failed to replicate this result, but did find that other evidence in the case was weighted differently by the mock jury. The discovery of some money in a car was regarded as more significant when there had been eyewitness evidence in the case, even if the evidence had been discredited. Instructions to beware of eyewitness testimony do reduce faith in it – but this wariness applies to accurate and inaccurate testimony equally, rather than sharpening discrimination between the two.

THE MESSAGE ITSELF

I turn now to the message itself and the presentation and ordering of arguments. An important general point to make is that listening to, understanding, and evaluating a continuous stream of information and arguments over hours or days is a difficult task for a human being. Research on how much people can take in from a lecture for example, shows that attention is unlikely to be sustained for more than 15 minutes or so before it wanders. The lesson for lecturers is to have a clear structure to the lecture, so that the inattentive listener can easily pick up the thread of the argument again. A common recommendation to lecturers is 'Say what you are going to say, say it, and then say what you have said'. Varied means of presenting information such as slides or a blackboard are also helpful in recapturing attention, and in setting out the framework the speaker is working through. The question and answer sequences of courtroom examination and cross-examination are probably rather a good way of breaking the information down into manageable segments, and holding or recapturing attention. Even better would be visual aids or other changes in format, rhythm, or style. But with extended testimony from one witness, and without a summary between witnesses of 'where we have got to and where we are going next' the flow of information in court can be extremely difficult to assimilate.

Information and arguments are taken in much better if the person listening is actively thinking about them, and trying to use the information or analyse the argument. This can be encouraged by the way in which information is prefaced and presented. The listener can be provided early on with a theme or schema into which the subsequent testimony can be integrated, acting as a framework for organizing new information. Research has found that 'story telling' is a powerful organizing device used by mock jurors in their deliberations. Information organization can also be helped by spelling out the conclusions that might be drawn, rather than leaving them implicit. Leaving the evidence to speak for itself is a dangerous strategy.

One strategy supported by psychological literature is that of forewarning a jury (or other audience) of an opponent's arguments and intentions. Obviously it would be counter-productive to dwell extensively on opposing arguments and make the case seem formidable. But refuting an argument or appeal before it is even presented is an effective way of 'inoculating' the audience. It seems to work by motivating the listener to think about counter-arguments while hearing the opposing evidence or appeal. This may be done by explicitly providing ready-made counter-arguments on specific points, or by stimulating the listener to generate them for him or herself.

Another strategy that research suggests would usually be effective is an appeal to emotion. It seems such appeals are as effective, if not more effective than rational appeals. The effect may, however, not be as lasting.

Lastly, there is the question of whether the order of presentation at a trial gives an advantage to the prosecution (or plaintiff) because they go first, or the defence because they go last; and whether strong arguments have more impact given early or saved until later – *primacy* versus *recency* effects. Unfortunately there is no clear-cut answer to this. Both effects are found. Although primacy effects were initially thought to be the general rule, many exceptions have been found. One circumstance in which recency prevails is where there is a long gap between the first and second message, so that the first one is to an important extent forgotten before the second one is presented. John Thibaut and Laurens Walker (1975) in their studies of legal procedure found dramatic recency effects in simulations of legal decision making. They attribute these principally to the adversarial structure of a trial, which causes decision makers to suspend judgement initially in anticipation of hearing contrary evidence from the other party. This would seem to favour the defence. However, Michael Saks and Reid Hastie (1978) conclude that in most states in the US order effects favour the prosecution, which has an extra recency opportunity, and which, within the stage of closing arguments has the advantage of inoculation and primacy as well, because the prosecution both opens and closes the final arguments, with the defence sandwiched in between.

THE MEDIUM

Most courtroom communication is of course verbal, usually oral but also written. Face-to-face oral communication is in itself more persuasive than written, taped or filmed communication. But against this, the change of pace introduced by using more than one channel of communication is likely to enhance the attention paid to the message. A listener who is having difficulty sustaining concentration on what is being said will wake up and pay attention again when a switch of medium is made to, say, videotape. Written information is also often better understood and remembered, probably because the reader can go back over passages. Some information may be just too complex to take in when presented orally. The Roskill Committee's (1986) recommendation of a move away from oral evidence in complex fraud cases has been strongly endorsed by psychologists. Psychological studies commissioned by the Committee showed, amongst other things, that graphs and diagrams greatly increased jurors' comprehension of time series information.

In addition, pictures, smells and sounds can make information much more vivid and this means that greater weight will be attached to it. The impact of photographs of injuries, for example, is well known. An empty whisky bottle reeking of alcohol as an exhibit has been recommended for its evocative power. These kinds of strategies can seem too much like tricks if overdone, but there is plenty of psychological evidence to confirm that they are very persuasive.

JURIES

Although the 'audience' in court will not always – nor indeed usually – be a jury, a great deal of special attention has been devoted to juries by psychologists. The amount of attention psychologists have given the jury is somewhat disproportionate to their role in the legal system, especially in the UK where juries play even less of a part than in the US and Canada. Despite all this attention there are considerable problems in drawing conclusions from jury studies. Real jury deliberations cannot be studied in North America or the UK. Even interrogating jurors after a case is not a real possibility in the UK. The best one can do is study 'mock' or 'shadow' jurors, who can never carry the same responsibility. Many mock juries have been composed of students, simply because these are easily come by in the universities and colleges where the research is carried out. And the presentation of a case to mock juries in many studies is a much impoverished version of an actual jury trial – perhaps a written summary, for example. All these limitations need not mean that the results of such studies do not tell us anything about actual juries. But it is important to have in mind the assumptions this extension makes: that a mock juror's processes of social perception and decision making are like an actual juror's; and that effects found in a context where mock jurors are given a written or tape-recorded summary of a case are not specific to that context. It is also worth noting that properly conducted simulations can be very involving and seem realistic to the participants. (After management bargaining and negotiation simulations, people who came into conflict in the simulation have been known to bear a lasting grudge.)

I first discuss jurors themselves and how their personal characteristics may affect their decisions, then how they operate as a group, and what is known about jury deliberation.

Juror characteristics

The information we have on the effects of individual characteristics of jurors comes partly from experiments with mock jurors, and partly from the experience of actual trials and 'scientific' jury selection – where psychologists have helped lawyers to select and eliminate jurors. 'Systematic' or 'scientific' jury selection is discussed later in this chapter.

Before discussing the effects of predispositions of individual jurors, it is important to stress that the most important aspect of any case with very few exceptions tends to be the strength of the evidence. It is only when there are weaknesses in the evidence that such factors as the beliefs and personality of jurors may come into play. Secondly, the process of deliberation tends to counteract bias introduced by the preconceptions of individual jurors. We are therefore looking at quite a minor aspect of courtroom processes in looking at individual juror bias.

A third point to emphasize is that it is in the nature of information processing that a juror will bring pre-existing conceptions and theories to bear on a case. As I discuss in more depth in the next chapter (on sentencing), incoming information has to be organized in some way for decision-making processes to get started at all. No juror has been raised in a barrel, and the preconceptions and theories he or she brings to bear on information presented at a trial will inevitably reflect personal experiences and other individual characteristics.

While this is inevitable, it is not always a cause for concern. Concern arises when jurors are suspected of, say, racial prejudice, or very authoritarian attitudes which might lead to an unfair predisposition to convict a particular defendant, or to convict in general. Conversely, jurors have been suspected of being overly sympathetic to some defendants, or in particular types of cases such as drunk driving cases. Racial bigotry is a good example of these kinds of biases. In one trial in the US in the 1950s, a 23-year-old black youth was charged with aiding and abetting the interstate transportation of a stolen car. After the trial, interviews were conducted with the jurors. It transpired that even though there was one black woman on the jury, two other jurors had been very open in voicing their prejudices during the deliberation, for example arguing for conviction because 'niggers are just no good'. Several other jurors admitted to the interviewer that they were prejudiced, making such comments as 'Niggers have to be taught to behave'. Although this example comes from the 1950s, there are plenty of more recent examples of effects of race, especially where the defendant accused of a sex crime is black and the victim is white.

In their book *Judging the Jury* (1986) Valerie Hans and Neil Vidmar make a very important point about how racial prejudice has its effect. Jurors may not be overtly prejudiced. Indeed they may make every effort to be impartial and fair, and yet bias may arise because they do not understand black language and culture, or misinterpret a defendant's demeanour as showing arrogance. As we saw in looking at O'Barr's work on language, quite subtle differences in speech style can make all the difference to how a witness is perceived and his or her testimony evaluated. How much greater might these effects on credibility be when the very different speech styles of some racial groups are used in courts?

As Hans and Vidmar illustrate, evidence can even become incomprehensible if there is no one on the jury familiar with the slang used. In one case, they describe how the phrase 'put in the dozens' was used by black witnesses testifying about events just before a killing. It never became clear during the trial what this meant. It was in fact very relevant to proving self-defence, since 'in the dozens' is an extreme form of verbal aggression. Evidence that the victim had 'put the defendant in the dozens' just before the killing effectively fell on deaf ears. Indeed, interviews after the trial showed that the jury found much of the evidence incomprehensible. The defendant's claim of self-defence did not succeed, despite a strong case, because neither the judge nor the jury were capable of understanding the testimony.

As well as specific biases such as racial prejudice, some jurors may be predisposed towards conviction or acquittal because of how authoritarian they are in personality. Authoritarianism is often thought of as a personality 'syndrome' associated with racism, political conservatism, punitiveness, and conviction proneness. There is some evidence that it is a stable feature of personality that shows up in a variety of different areas of the individual's behaviour.

One area where it appears to operate is in trials in the United States where the death penalty is a possibility. Jurors for such trials have to be 'death qualified' – that is, they must have no difficulty about convicting on the evidence because of their moral beliefs about the death penalty. It has become apparent from several American studies that jurors who are willing to convict in these circumstances are not only in favour of the death penalty, but also biased in favour of conviction, and are likely to be less sympathetic than other juries towards blacks and other racial minorities.

Systematic jury selection

'Systematic' or 'scientific' jury selection using social science techniques has been developed in the US where jury selection is a much more prominent feature of trials than in the UK. In the US a pre-trial questioning period called the *voir dire* is a routine preliminary to every jury trial. It can take as long as 49 days as it did for the trial of the Hillside Strangler in Los Angeles. But usually it is much briefer: as short as 20 minutes. During the *voir dire* prospective jurors are questioned by the judge and/or attorneys, and may be eliminated from the jury. The judge may dismiss jurors that he or she determines would not be impartial; or attorneys may exercise a specified number of 'peremptory challenges'. These are challenges for which no reasons need be given. The number available varies depending on the seriousness of the case. A typical number is six, but for very serious crimes 12 or more may be allowed.

A detailed and fascinating account of 'scientific' jury selection is to be found in Hans and Vidmar (1986). They describe an antitrust case that was tried in 1980. The jury awarded MCI Communication Corporation $600 million, to be paid by the American Telephone and Telegraph Company (AT&T). This award was tripled for punitive purposes (automatic in antitrust cases) to the record sum of $1.8 billion. Their extraordinary success was, according to Hans and Vidmar, not really a surprise for the attorneys for the winning side, because they had, before the trial, engaged jury researchers who used social science techniques to predict how jurors would react to the evidence and to help select the jurors who would be most favourable to MCI.

As is the usual procedure in 'scientific' jury selection, the mainstay of the process was a local survey carried out by telephone and personal interview, covering the geographical area from which a jury would eventually be recruited. Citizens were asked questions designed to reveal whether they would be likely to side with MCI or with AT&T, if they were themselves jurors. At the same time their demographic characteristics were recorded – age, sex, occupation, political affiliation, and so on. On this basis, a demographic profile of individuals favourable and unfavourable to the case was developed, and it was later used to help select and reject the actual prospective jurors.

The next step was to invite selected individuals of varying sympathy towards MCI to attend a meeting (for which they were paid) on one of three successive evenings. At each meeting a mock jury of eight was made up and observed a mini-trial in which the attorneys presented an abbreviated version of the case for each side, and then deliberated on the case while the researchers observed and listened from behind a one-way mirror.

The procedure provided valuable information on how jurors might react to the case. For example, AT&T was required by law to share its long lines with other communication companies, and the mock jurors were told this. On the first evening it was discovered that the mock jurors became engaged in a heated debate about whether the law was a fair one: why should the company have to share its lines with competitors? The debate was disturbing to the attorneys. It suggested sympathy for the moral position of AT&T could arise for non-legal reasons. The next night with a new mock jury they emphasized that it was not up to the jury to decide whether they personally thought the law was fair – but to apply the law as it stood. This did the trick. Jurors that night did not have much difficulty accepting the law.

A second valuable lesson was learned during the mock jury sessions. At the first evening, the attorney representing MCI's argument said they had lost $100 million in profit because of AT&T's monopolistic practices. The mock jury subsequently awarded precisely this amount in damages. The next night the attorneys experimented with not mentioning a sum, and the mock jury awarded $900 million!

Hans and Vidmar add that the jury research team may have been *too* successful this time. The award of $600 million was overturned on appeal and reduced to $37.8 million.

It would be essential to carry out special research for each particular trial. Who would make a 'good' juror has turned out to vary from case to case and from one geographical area to another. Psychologists have invariably found that behaviour can most accurately be predicted from specific information rather than more general attitudes, and responses to a trial are no exception. A *local* survey asking questions relevant to the *particular* case is critical to this system of jury selection. The selection procedure sometimes also takes into account what is known about jury dynamics to select a jury with an eye to who is likely to act as foreperson, and who is likely to yield to others. Thus, for one trial concerning anti-Vietnam war demonstrations, a low-authoritarian jury was sought by the defence. A particular low-authoritarian, college-educated white woman seemed a favourable foreperson, and so potential rivals for leadership (high status males) were eliminated. Conversely, because relatively low status authoritarians were likely to yield to others, two 'rednecks' were not challenged, as it was thought they were unlikely to do much harm.

Similar methods to those described above have been used in a number of other trials in North America. The earliest were trials with political overtones, and indeed the method of using a local survey was developed for the defence side in the 1972 conspiracy trial in which seven anti-Vietnam war protesters were on trial – the 'Harrisburg seven'. The outcome of the trial was a victory for the defendants.

Systematic jury selection has coincided with winning in a growing number of cases. However, there are reasons to remain sceptical about some of the more extravagant claims made for it. It is most suitable for cases where the jurors' beliefs dispose them one way or the other, such as cases with political overtones. It will not help in every type of case; and if the evidence is very strong or very weak, no amount of jury selection or refinement of advocacy techniques will overcome that. Psychologists obviously cannot definitely predict how a juror will react, only help to improve the probability of a favourable reaction if there is a range of different attitudes and backgrounds among potential jurors.

A study in a federal district court indicated that the exclusion of certain jurors can make a difference to trial outcome. In 12 (real) trials, the jurors who had been challenged (by either side) sat in court for the trial. The researchers interviewed them after the trial, and compared this information with information from interviews with the real jurors. They were able to work out what an initial vote would have been if the challenged jurors had been allowed to remain on the jury, and compared this with what actually happened. They concluded that in at least two or three of the trials the verdict would have been different had the challenged jurors not been excluded.

Since the evidence in the case is what is crucial, simulations trying out different ways of presenting the evidence, as was done in the MCI case described above, can potentially be very informative. There is no way of learning for sure whether the real jury will react in the same way as the mock jury, but the insights provided can be immensely useful in helping to refine a trial strategy.

On balance, then, there is some scope for systematic jury selection and other social scientific techniques to affect the outcome of a trial. But this scope is limited, and the methods are subject to considerable error. Several psychologists have rightly criticized the use of the label 'scientific' jury selection. As Hans and Vidmar write: '"Scientific" creates a mystique, an impression of accuracy and precision, that the techniques cannot deliver'.

The competence of jurors

One eminent jurist (Glanville Williams) has described the jury as 'a group of twelve men of average ignorance'. Jury verdicts, especially acquittals, are sometimes regarded as perverse or simply incomprehensible by judges and other lawyers. Juries, it is feared, may not understand the law, take in the facts of the case, or follow instructions from the judge. How justified are those fears?

There is no doubt that cases do arise where the jury is baffled by the evidence, or confused about the law, or ignores the law and brings in a verdict that is based on the jurors' own sense of justice. However, these are probably a small proportion of all cases. Because jurors (and judges) have much more readily been interviewed in the United States than in the UK we have much more information from there.

In the landmark study *The American Jury* (1966) carried out by Kalven and Zeisel in the United States, judges and jury disagreed on 22 per cent of the verdicts, but these were not cases where the evidence was particularly complex or difficult. The researchers concluded that it was not jury incompetence, but other factors that led to these disagreements. If a defendant had no prior record, for example, juries were more likely to give the benefit of the doubt than were judges. Where the case was marginal, juries were more inclined to err on the side of leniency.

Several instances were found where the juries deviated from the law. In many of these instances a jury was more sympathetic towards a claim of self-defence than a judge would be, such as where there was a pattern of wife abuse. Hans and Vidmar cite a more recent Canadian case where this occurred. Jane Stafford shot and killed her common-law husband in 1982. She had been beaten and abused by him over five years. Before then he had abused two previous wives and also children. He was a hefty bully, and was also a sexual sadist. Despite the fact that Stafford confessed to having killed him while he was unconscious from drinking, the jury verdict, to everyone's surprise, was 'not guilty'.

In the UK, Baldwin and McConville gathered the views of judges, prosecuting solicitors, defence solicitors and the police on several hundred jury verdicts. The main sample consisted of 370 jury trials in Birmingham. Judges expressed 'serious doubts' about as many as 36 per cent of the acquittals, and in 3.2 per cent of convictions a great deal of uncertainty was expressed. Baldwin and McConville were especially concerned by the questionable convictions but they found no clear pattern to explain why these disagreements arose. They are much more negative about the competence of juries than Kalven and Zeisel – and indeed than Hans and Vidmar.

However, in the absence of any clear explanation of the doubtful verdicts, it is difficult to come to any conclusion beyond that judges, police and solicitors are often surprised or dismayed at jury verdicts. Of course judges and lawyers themselves sometimes disagree. While judges viewed 36 per cent of acquittals as seriously doubtful, the prosecuting solicitor, for example, expressed serious doubt in 26 per cent; the defence solicitor in 10 per cent; and the police in 44 per cent of acquittals.

There has also been concern about whether jurors can understand the evidence presented in fraud cases or other complex evidence such as medical or ballistic evidence. The Roskill Committee (1986) concluded that little of the complex information presented to jurors in fraud trials would be retained and that this could adversely affect their decisions. The Committee commissioned the Medical Research Council Applied Psychology Unit (APU) at Cambridge to carry out research into the capacity of the general public to understand parts of the trial process. The studies, published as part of the Committee's report, showed that quite minor innovations in procedure could make a substantial difference to what was understood. For example, providing a glossary of technical terms significantly improved comprehension and recall of a judicial summing up taken from a fraud case. Changes in the format of a summary of an argument almost doubled understanding of the debate that preceded it. The APU's findings point to reforms in the way evidence is presented, and especially, as already mentioned, a move away from oral presentation. It is, however, questionable whether the research points to the conclusion recommended by Roskill, that a special tribunal should replace the jury trial in complex fraud cases. This would require research into how much is typically understood by the jury in a fraud trial; and how it compares with the understanding of other groups of people who might make up a tribunal. The APU researchers concentrated on ways of making information more readily understood by jurors. As they explicitly state at the end of their report:

> None of the present projects has sought to estimate the amount understood in a typical trial. Instead the emphasis within the project has been on the comparative effects of changing the way information is presented to comparable groups of people. (Roskill Report, 1986)

Comprehension of instructions

An area where it is possible to make much more definite statements is that of juror comprehension of instructions. There is ample evidence that jurors have trouble with specific instructions. There are two sources of this trouble: one is the language in which complex legal concepts are presented to jurors; and the other is the inherent impossibility of certain instructions – for example, to disregard particular pieces of information. Researchers in both the United States and the UK have applied what is known about the comprehensibility of language to legal material. It has been amply demonstrated that difficult and obscure language can very often be translated into a much more comprehensible form without losing precision (see the discussion of using clear language in Chapter 6). Psychologists in America have applied these psycholinguistic findings specifically to improving the comprehensibility of pattern jury instructions. Pattern instructions are standardized instructions that judges use to explain the law to jurors, thus avoiding the problems of wrong instructions giving rise to appeals. The same general linguistic rules outlined in Chapter 6 apply here also. For example, Hans and Vidmar quote the following rewrite of the California instruction on negligence for civil cases. The original runs as follows:

> One test that is helpful in determining whether or not a person was negligent is to ask and answer whether or not, if a person of ordinary prudence had been in the same situation and possessed of the same knowledge, he would have foreseen or anticipated that someone might have been injured as a result of his action or inaction. If such a result from certain conduct would be foreseeable by a person of ordinary prudence with like knowledge and in like situation, and if the conduct reasonably could be avoided, then not to avoid it would be negligence.

This horror was rewritten by Robert and Vera Charrow (1979) as follows:

> In order to decide whether or not the defendant was negligent, there is a test you can use. Consider how a reasonably careful person would have acted in the same situation. Specifically, in order to find the defendant negligent, you would have to answer 'yes' to the following two questions:
>
> 1. Would a reasonably careful person have realized in advance that someone might be injured as a result of the defendant's conduct?
>
> And,
>
> 2. Could a reasonably careful person have avoided behaving as the defendant did? If your answer to both these questions is 'yes', then the defendant is negligent. You can use the same test in deciding whether the plaintiff was negligent.

The sentences are shorter; unusual words and phrases ('prudence', 'possessed of knowledge') have been removed, as have homonyms ('like', 'certain') and synonyms ('foreseen or anticipated'). Negatives are avoided, and the whole instruction is set out in a series of easily grouped, logical steps. Not surprisingly, research conducted to compare the two versions showed that jurors' comprehension was dramatically better with the revised version.

It is not only jurors, of course, who have difficulty with the concept of negligence. Coutts (1960), referring to the confusion surrounding legal use of causal language, writes:

> one has a sneaking sympathy for the Irish High Court Judge who evaded the task of explaining the tangled rules of 'last opportunity' to the jury in a running down action by asking them to answer 'the simple question: which car hit the other first?'

A number of other suggestions have been made by North American psychologists that would make it easier for jurors to remember the relevant facts and apply the law correctly. One is that juror instructions should be given before as well as (or rather than) at the end of a trial. The instructions could be given to the jury in written form as well as orally, and they could then refer to them at any time. Allowing juries to take notes would also be helpful. All these recommendations would go towards helping the juror with the cognitive demands of the task without introducing interference or bias.

The other side to juror instructions is whether, having understood them, jurors follow them. As I suggested above, this can be impossible for the best intentioned juror if the instructions concern disregarding information, or using it only in certain restricted ways. One interesting study illustrating this used as subjects people called for jury duty in Chicago and St Louis. A tape-recorded trial of a civil case was played to them, and their task was to decide damages. Some of the simulated jurors learned that the defendant was insured, while others heard that he was not insured. Amongst those who learned he was insured, half heard the judge give an instruction to disregard the information. The results were as follows: jurors told there was no insurance awarded an average of $33,000. Jurors told there was insurance and *not* told to disregard this information awarded an average of $37,000. Jurors told to disregard the information about insurance awarded an average of $46,000. It seems the instruction had the opposite effect to that intended. Study of the deliberations showed that the jurors had done their best to follow the instruction. Either they did not discuss the insurance at all, or, if it came up, other jurors said they should not be considering it. The information thus seems to have affected their judgement in quite a subtle way, and without their being aware of it. (See pp. 61–67 for further discussion of how we can be mistaken about what is influencing our decisions.)

Juries do not decide on damage awards in Britain, but they are instructed to disregard evidence in other types of cases, and similar problems may be expected. One piece of information that can be impossible to delete from people's minds is, of course, evidence of prior record. Psychological studies have confirmed that prior record information is very powerful and its use cannot be confined by conscious effort to assessing the credibility of the defendant, rather than more directly assessing the probability of guilt.

Jury deliberations

Here again most of the information we have is North American, partly because juries feature much more prominently in the United States, and are used in a wider range of decisions. They therefore attract more research interest. It is also because it has been possible to interview jurors after trials and learn something about what went on in the jury room. This provides extremely valuable information both in itself and against which to check research findings with simulated juries.

One often-quoted conclusion of Kalven and Zeisel's jury project is that 'The deliberation process might well be likened to what the developer does for an exposed film; it brings out the picture but the outcome is predetermined'. There is truth in this. Verdicts of mock juries can very often be predicted from a pre-deliberation vote. However, it seems there are several valuable functions served by deliberation. One is, quite simply, increased accuracy of memory for the evidence. The pooled memories of 12 jurors are an improvement on one individual memory. One study showed that juries collectively accurately remembered 90 per cent of the facts and 80 per cent of the judge's instructions in a case. This compared very favourably with individual mock jurors' recollections.

A second beneficial effect of deliberation is to help neutralize the effects of pre-existing biases. As well as more long-standing beliefs and prejudices, deliberation dissipates the effects of negative moods that may have been created during the trial. For example, annoying interruptions and dogmatic lectures from the judge in one study were found to create more general negative feelings among mock jurors, including their feelings toward the defendant. However, these effects disappeared or were at least reduced after the deliberation phase.

Not surprisingly, the most probable verdict after deliberation is that of the majority before deliberation. But the relationship between individual jurors' initial views and the eventual verdict is not straightforward. An important finding is that leniency tends to win out. In one study individual views were gathered from a pool of mock jurors, and six-person mock juries were composed such that half the juries had an initial 4:2 majority in favour of a guilty verdict, and half had a 4:2 majority in favour of not guilty. Where the initial majority favoured 'not guilty', only one out of 18 juries reached a 'guilty' verdict. But where the majority initially favoured 'guilty', only seven out of 19 reached a 'guilty' verdict. Seven verdicts were 'not guilty', and five juries could not reach a unanimous verdict in the time allowed. The shift is not always in this direction, however. When the case against the defendant is strong, discussion of the evidence leads to a shift in the other direction towards jurors perceiving a greater degree of guilt. A minority of one, despite Henry Fonda's persuasive performance in the film *Twelve Angry Men*, has virtually no chance of winning support. Thus, the process of deliberation polarizes the views of the group, but there is a bias toward the lenient end.

Norbert Kerr and Robert Bray (1982), after reviewing the evidence for this 'leniency' bias in deliberations, raise the interesting possibility that it may lie behind the frequent finding that juries tend to be, if anything, more lenient in their verdicts than individual judges would be. Individual jurors are more likely to be pro-conviction before deliberation than they are after it. It would be interesting to know how close individual jurors' *initial* positions are to those of judges and other lawyers.

The stages of deliberation. The first task of a jury is usually to select a foreperson. Although this is generally done quickly and with the ready agreement of everyone, it is a rather structured decision. The social structure of the jury mirrors the status of its members in the outside world. Thus, males of higher occupational status are more likely to become foreperson than are women or members from occupations with lower social status.

Once discussion is under way, different members of the jury will speak with different frequency. Again, this is partly a question of status but it is also a reflection of the emerging line-up of factions within a jury. The larger the faction to which a member belongs, the less often he or she is likely to contribute to the discussion. It also depends on jury size: experiments with six-person juries have shown that usually everyone speaks, whereas in a 12-person jury, sometimes individual jurors make no contribution to discussions at all.

Various patterns have been discerned in the path that deliberations take. (See, for example, Hastie, Penrod and Pennington's book *Inside the Jury*, 1983.) An important determinant of how it will go seems to be the manner in which and stage at which votes are taken. Taking a vote early on seems to hasten deliberations on from the preliminaries to a stage of conflict resolution. In addition, simulated juries using secret ballots are more likely to end up as hung juries. However, it could be that secret ballots are used when there is more disagreement anyway.

Hastie and his colleagues distinguished between 'evidence driven' deliberations and 'verdict driven' deliberations. With simulated juries, 'verdict driven' deliberations often began with a public ballot. Clear alignments of support emerged quickly and statements were frequently made concerning preference for a particular verdict. In contrast, 'evidence driven' deliberations began with a general review of the evidence, and attempts to develop an agreed joint version of events. Polling occurred much later in the deliberations.

In summary, fascinating though these studies of deliberation processes are, it seems that the impact of deliberation on verdicts is limited. Most verdicts can be predicted from the positions that jurors take at the end of the trial and before deliberation begins. None the less, as I have already suggested, deliberations can serve important functions in the pooling of the collective memories and knowledge of jurors, and in reducing certain kinds of bias. Also, it may be here that the source of the bias toward leniency among jurors as compared with judges lies. When a case is sufficiently questionable to have raised doubt in a minority's minds, they may actually win out against a majority initially in favour of convicting.

In conclusion . . .

A psychological perspective on what goes on in court emphasizes several processes of persuasion and influence, and cognitive processes of understanding and using information. Research on the credibility of witnesses has shown how important are language style and the appearance of confidence. Both may mislead the listener. Language style may invoke misleading stereotypes and limit comprehension. Confidence may be a poor indication of accuracy. The impact of evidence is increased if it is vivid and presented in a comprehensible way. The cognitive tasks of listening to and evaluating evidence can be greatly assisted (or inhibited) by the way it is presented and structured and this in turn affects how the information is used in arriving at a decision.

Research on the dynamics and competence of juries has produced some insights, but it is always important to have in mind the limitations of research on mock jurors. Systematic jury selection, while spectacularly successful in some cases, has limited application. It is also worth remembering that, in Britain especially, the jury trial is a comparatively rare event in criminal justice. About 98 per cent of criminal cases are dealt with in the lower courts. The jury in civil cases survives in Northern Ireland, but has in practice disappeared in the rest of the UK except in libel cases.

References

Baldwin, J. and McConville, M. (1979) *Jury Trials*. Oxford: Clarendon Press.

Charrow, R. and Charrow, V. (1979) Making legal language understandable: A psycholinguistic study of jury instructions. *Columbia Law Review, 79,* 1306–1374.

Coutts, J.A. (1960) Review of 'Causation in the Law' by H.L.A Hart and A.M. Honore. *Modern Law Review 23,* 708–709.

*Hans, V.P. and Vidmar, N. (1986) *Judging the Jury*. New York: Plenum.

*Hastie, R., Penrod, S. and Pennington, N. (1983) *Inside the Jury*. Cambridge, Massachusetts: Harvard University Press.

Kalven, H. and Zeisel, H. (1966) *The American Jury*. Boston: Little Brown.

*Kerr, N.L. and Bray, R.M. (ed.) (1982) *The Psychology of the Courtroom*. New York: Academic Press.

*O'Barr, W.M. (1982) *Linguistic Evidence: Language, Power and Strategy in the Courtroom*. New York: Academic Press.

Roskill, Lord P.C. (1986) *Fraud Trials Committee Report*. London: HMSO.

*Saks, M.J. and Hastie, R. (1978) *Social Psychology in Court*. New York: Van Nostrand Rheinhold.

Thibaut, J. and Walker, L. (1975) *Procedural Justice: A Psychological Analysis*. New Jersey: Hillsdale.

Further reading

Publications marked with an asterisk (*) above.

Chapter 4

Sentencing

The previous chapter looked at the processes of persuasion and understanding information in court. Much of what was said there applies to sentencing too. The judge or magistrate is presented with information designed to persuade, some of it specifically designed to persuade about sentencing, and must reach a decision on this basis. However, judges and magistrates are often very experienced at their jobs. Experience has interesting implications for how people take decisions. This chapter applies research on decision making to the sentencer's task.

THE SENTENCER'S TASK

Sentencing is a type of task sometimes called 'open' problem solving. An open problem is one without clear, unambiguous criteria for a correct solution. The competing and often conflicting goals of sentencing mean that the criteria for right decisions are not clear. Added to this, sentencing is at least partly a moral decision. The moral rightness of the decision may lie in how the sentence fits the crime, rather than its further consequences, such as deterrence, or rehabilitation.

From a psychological perspective the task of sentencing has a lot in common with such tasks as making a move in chess, medical diagnosis, an aircraft pilot's decision whether to divert to another airport and weather forecasting. There are obvious limits to these comparisons. But in each setting, a decision on a course of action has to be taken on the basis of whatever information is available. The decision maker must select one of a number of possible alternative courses of action; there is a certain amount of time to think about what to do (that is, the choice is not an immediate reaction); and there is a significant element of uncertainty about whether the decision is the 'best' one, either because the information available is itself of a patchy or probabilistic nature, or because of the decision maker's own cognitive limitations as a human being. Because sentencing is partly a moral decision without clear and obvious aims, it is particularly difficult to know whether or not a sentencing decision was the 'right' one. It is often rather more obvious whether decisions about piloting aircraft, diagnosing disease, or weather forecasting were right or wrong.

Rather little of the research that has been done on the psychology of decision making has looked specifically at criminal sentencing. This is partly because it has not been easy to obtain the necessary access for empirical research. Much of the applied work in this area has been concerned with engineering psychology. In particular I shall draw on Christopher Wickens's book *Engineering Psychology and Human Performance* (1984), and I shall be referring to ideas about the degree to which responses are automatic rather than reflective that were developed in the context of safety systems for nuclear power plants. The leap from such contexts to sentencing must obviously be speculative, but there are indications that common factors are at work. Some general features of decision making are likely to be common between sentencing and other reflective and complex decisions of choice, diagnosis or prediction.

Sentencing as a cognitive skill

Cognitive psychologists often envisage the process of deciding what to do as falling on a continuum according to how automatic it is. Towards the 'automatic' end of the continuum, the individual already has in memory a category into which the event or other stimulus can be rapidly classified, and a response that is automatically triggered by that category. In other words the response is skill-based. The action is an immediate response to a perceived stimulus – slamming on the brakes, for example. Towards the middle of the continuum, a situation that has never been encountered before can be classified as an example of a class, and action is based on a set of rules (also in memory) of the 'If A then do B' type. At the other end of the continuum rules and categories do not already exist in the person's repertoire to cope with the new situation, and the decision on action is taken only after the alternatives and their likely consequences have been worked through on the basis of more general knowledge. Totally new problems requiring a novel solution would be dealt with at this time-consuming level.

Sentencing, the vast majority of the time, will most likely fall somewhere in the middle to automatic zone (as indeed will the other types of medical, piloting, and weather-forecasting decisions mentioned above). The possibility of responding toward the automatic end of the continuum depends on categories and rules having been built up through experience and practice – the essence of the development of any skill. Less experienced judges or magistrates are likely to be making decisions in a less automatic, more time-consuming way.

An Australian study by Jeanette Lawrence and Ross Homel compared experienced and novice magistrates, and found clear differences of the kind I have suggested. The two groups used different frames of reference and made different inferences. Lawrence and Homel comment on one example as follows:

> Expert One's attention to detail was sustained in the kinds of inference he made about this shopstealer and his general expectations about her kind. . . . he drew his own conclusions about Sarah's personal problems and emotional state, and her intention to steal the goods. He had a *patterned expectation which was activated as soon as the charge was read*. . . . She would be an ordinary shopstealer. . . . 'She's undoubtedly married. Yes and probably got two children, and I'll be told all this later. There's an immediate suspicion that things aren't good at home and that she's in fact a repressed housewife. . . . (Lawrence and Homel, 1986; italics added)

Judges have described sentencing as a process that would fall towards the 'automatic' skill-based end rather than the 'from scratch' end. For example, researchers at the Centre for Criminological Research at Oxford report, on the basis of interviews with 25 judges, that:

> Only a minority . . . regarded sentencing as a matter of principles and reasoned conclusions. Most judges described it as an intuitive process, using such terms as 'instinct', 'hunch' and 'feeling'. (Ashworth *et al.*, 1984)

This is a consistent thread in writings about and by judges. In *Law and the Modern Mind* (1930) for example, Jerome Frank made much of the importance of judges' 'hunches', quoting an article by Judge Hutcheson entitled 'The Judgement Intuitive: the function of the hunch in judicial decisions', concluding that 'the way in which the judge gets his hunches is the key to the judicial process'. Frank was concerned with the judges' decisions about matters other than sentencing, but the general point applies. The more automatic and the less consciously puzzled over a decision is, the more one could expect it to be experienced and described as 'instinct' or 'hunch'.

It is worth emphasizing that 'automatic' does not have to mean 'simple' or 'crude'. Highly complex stimuli may be rapidly classified into a category. A skilled doctor, for example, may immediately recognize a syndrome and identify the appropriate treatment. Moreover, he or she is not only likely to be quicker, but also likely to be more consistently accurate than an inexperienced medical student working at a less automatic level. Also, there is no reason why a decision such as sentencing should fall neatly and consistently at any particular level of automaticity. For example, a certain point in the decision might be reached fairly quickly and automatically, and then other aspects puzzled about at some length. David Thomas (1979) breaks custodial sentencing down into primary and secondary decisions, where the primary decision sets a tariff range, within which the secondary decision applies individual aggravating and mitigating factors. But sentencing is often undertaken over and over again by a person of some experience, in relation to cases that fall into types and categories that the sentencer has seen before. It is therefore very probable that the task is accomplished largely by classifying cases comparatively automatically as typical of some class, and responding to them on that basis.

Why not ask the sentencers?

One would not, however, necessarily expect a judge or magistrate to be able to articulate what categories and rules are being used to achieve their decision. The point about 'hunches' and 'intuitions' is that the decision maker is not directly aware of a reasoning process whereby the choice or decision was arrived at. What one gets when one asks a judge for instance to describe how he or she arrives at a sentence is not necessarily going to be a very good description of the cognitive processes involved. When people are asked to explain how they make decisions and diagnoses, what they are able to describe is seriously limited by the fact that much, if not all, of the process is simply not available to them through introspection. Reasons publicly given for a sentence may be even less of a guide, for these are to such a large degree justifications.

What tends to happen is that their answers (quite unintentionally) exaggerate the extent to which decisions are consciously reasoned over in elaborate detail. An important article in this area was published by Richard Nisbett and Timothy Wilson in 1977, entitled 'Telling more than we can know: verbal reports on mental processes'. As its title suggests, the article sets out to show that what are presented as accounts of mental processes are often not accurate accounts. People are simply not aware of the factors influencing them and the strategies they use. When a motor mechanic was asked how he diagnosed a fault, his reply resembled a few pages from a manual, and made excellent sense. However, the actual process was far more intuitive and skill-based than his account would suggest.

In their influential book *Human Inference: Strategies and Shortcomings of Social Judgment* (1980) Richard Nisbett and Lee Ross describe a series of studies exploring how people explain judgements they have made. By setting up experiments, it is possible to obtain an 'objective' measure of the degree to which, taken as a group, people's judgements or decisions were influenced by various factors; and then compare this with people's subjective accounts. For example, in one experiment subjects were asked to predict how much shock they would take in an experiment on the effects of intense electric shocks. For some subjects the description of the proposed experiment included a reassurance that the shocks would do no permanent damage. For others, no such reassurance was included. Subjects who received the reassurance were afterwards asked whether it had affected their predictions of the amount of shock they would take; and subjects who had not received the reassurance were asked whether it *would* have affected their predictions had it been included. It now becomes possible to compare what the subjects *said* about the effect of the reassurance on their predictions with the *actual* effect (or absence of it).

In fact, analysis of the predictions made by the two groups showed that there was no significant difference between them: the inclusion of the reassurance appeared to have had no effect. Yet a majority of subjects in the first group reported that it *had* affected their prediction; and those in the second group were inclined to say that it would have done so had it been included.

The basis of sentencer's accounts

Across a wide range of contexts, this series of studies showed that people's reports on the causes of their behaviour, choices and decisions can be very inaccurate indeed. What seems to be happening is that people's accounts often depend on their own *theories* about the processes concerned, rather than direct experience of them. As Nisbett and Ross explained, we have theories about why we answer telephones, how we solve problems, and why we open refrigerators, and these theories are usually correct. So a person who solves a problem by applying an algorithm, and then says he or she solved it by applying the algorithm, is right. But there are other areas where, as the experiment outlined above showed, these theories seem to be wrong, and lead people to believe they were influenced by factors that actually had no effect.

Since there is so much discussion of sentencing aims, criteria, and options, and since reasons for a sentence are often given, one would expect sentencers to have quite elaborate theories about what factors they take into account, and how they weigh these to make their decision. In some studies it does seem that judges' accounts of how they take decisions are better regarded as a statement of their theories than as a description of actual decision processes.

A study by Vladimir Konecni and Ebbe Ebbesen (1982) used a variety of different methods to study judges' sentencing in San Diego. The results were different for each of the different methods used. For example, they found that when eight judges were interviewed as if for a newspaper article they emphasized (as one might expect) that sentencing decisions are difficult and complex and that each case is different. The interviews indicated that judges take many factors into account when deciding a sentence, and more than a dozen 'important' factors were specifically mentioned. However, the results of the researchers' analysis of court records of actual cases led them to conclude that in fact a very few factors influence sentencing – notably, severity of crime, prior record, and the probation officer's recommendation. In this sense the decisions appeared to be quite simple. They write: 'the fact that judges *talk* about numerous factors . . . may have nothing to do with the causal factors that control their decisions'. Indeed, as these authors point out, with only around five minutes per sentencing hearing, and batches of 10–15 files received for decision the following day, there is simply not time for much deliberation. Whether or not one wholly accepts Konecni and Ebbesen's interpretation of their results, it is clear that the judges' introspective accounts of how they sentence did not provide a good model for predicting their actual decisions.

Pruning the decision tree

Whether a sentencer is an experienced and skilled regular, or a newcomer or occasional decision maker, he or she will have to employ simplifying strategies of some kind to cope with the task. As Donald Broadbent (1984) points out, even the comparatively simple everyday task of deciding in what order to carry out 10 jobs would take 20 hours if every possible order were to be checked (allowing 20 milliseconds for checking each one). In the most ordinary of tasks, the successive branching of different possibilities makes the tree of consequences too complex to be approached in this comprehensive way. The intelligent approach is, as Broadbent puts it, to look for ways of pruning the tree – or in other words, of cutting down the number of alternatives considered. The most rational methods of simplification will involve using pre-existing knowledge. Strategies of pruning a problem might include for example, testing the most probable hypothesis first; employing readily available memories; and matching the present problem to similar previous ones.

Biases

Although 'tree pruning' is rational in itself, the strategies employed may not always produce the best result. A considerable amount of research has been done indicating that humans use rules of thumb that can simplify a complex task and make it less demanding on cognitive resources such as memory and attention. However, these same rules of thumb can introduce systematic biases. For example, a number of biases in intuitive use of statistics, probabilities, and causal influences are well established.

Catherine Fitzmaurice and Ken Pease have speculated at some length about the possible implications of this research for sentencing in the chapter 'Cognitive Errors and Judges' in their book *The Psychology of Judicial Sentencing* (1986). One bias they discuss is a tendency to see causes of behaviour as lying within *individuals* rather than the *situation* in which they find themselves. This is a consistent finding in a number of different contexts. Where sentencing is concerned this bias could mean that sentencers are prone to give insufficient weight to situational pressures on the offender and to exaggerate the extent to which the offender could have controlled his or her behaviour.

A second bias, known as 'false consensus bias', is the tendency to believe that others agree with one's own view more than they in fact do. A third is the 'knew-it-all-along' effect, where with hindsight people exaggerate what they could have predicted. Fitzmaurice and Pease acknowledge that the necessary research has not been done to investigate these effects in sentencing. However, they point out that judges do tend to locate the causes of criminality in the individual, citing as an example Ashworth and colleagues' interviews with judges mentioned above. They point out that judges in this same study were also on the whole confident that they could identify informed public opinion – which the majority believed coincided with their own opinions.

Expected patterns

For a sentencing decision to be possible at all, the incoming information has to be organized in some way, and some form of provisional structure imposed on it. As we saw in the example from Lawrence and Homel's research, a working hypothesis about the nature of the case is likely to be formed at an early stage and guide the processing of new information. This is a valuable strategy for organizing information, but it has its drawbacks. Research has sometimes found a tendency to process information in such a way that allows one to hold on to a working hypothesis. The working hypothesis may itself reflect biases arising from simplification strategies, such as a tendency to attend only to a few critical features, or to adopt a hypothesis that comes easily to mind, perhaps because a similar instance has occurred recently. Once an initial hypothesis has been formulated, the decision maker is likely to seek confirming information and avoid disconfirming information, in what has been described as 'cognitive tunnel vision'. Dealing with negative information and reformulating hypotheses requires time and a much higher degree of cognitive effort. Fitting new information into an existing decision frame need not mean distorting or denying the basic 'facts'. Several interpretative slants on the same facts may be possible.

The decision maker's task in complex decision making such as sentencing is simplified if there are patterns of correlated features in the event or case to be categorized and responded to. John Payne (1980) has shown this in the context of parole decisions. When parole officers repeatedly encounter correlated clusters of attributes in the cases they consider, they are better able to classify cases. The disadvantage is that cases that do not quite fit into an expected pattern may none the less be forced into a category rather than treated as something unusual. Payne, for example, noticed that when a parolee has some, but not all, the attributes of the 'typical' drug offender, he or she will be readily categorized as one for parole purposes.

Idiosyncrasies in sentencing

Another disadvantage of skill-based decision making can be that decisions become more idiosyncratic, since sentencers' experiences, on the basis of which they acquire their expertise, will differ. Lawrence and Homel cite a very experienced magistrate in their study who described the tendency to work from well-established schemata but who also expressed concern about the dangers of routinely operating on well-used patterns. The problem is closely linked with the question of individual differences between sentencers, which I return to below.

Feedback to sentencers

Another disadvantage of skill-based decision making can be that debased should be feedback to sentencers on the consequences of their decisions; yet they are in a peculiar position here. They are rather unlikely ever to know the outcome of particular decisions, and there is unlikely to be any clear criterion of a 'right' or 'wrong' sentence. Such feedback as they do receive tends to be systematically negative, and to relate mostly to other sentencers' decisions: the flow of re-offenders appearing before them provides continual evidence of the ineffectiveness of sentences in altering behaviour. Appeals are relatively rare. It is known from research on a range of professional decision makers that clear and quick feedback is an essential antidote to overconfidence in the correctness of judgements and predictions. Professionals in general are prone to overestimate their own level of right decisions. About the only exception to the rule of overconfidence seems to be weather forecasters, who of course are forced to face up to feedback on their forecasts. Indeed, this is part of the process of calibrating their forecasts: on 70 per cent of occasions on which they say there is a 70 per cent chance of rain, it should in fact rain. They are thence accurate in their estimates of their own accuracy.

Extensive feedback to sentencers on the consequences of large numbers of individual sentences is unlikely to be feasible. But feedback of a more general type, on sentences being awarded, or reconviction rates, may go some way towards providing a sense of the effectiveness or otherwise of sentences (given particular aims) and the practices of other sentencers.

Information on the practice of other sentencers is especially important for minimizing disparity. But judges may not even have an accurate picture of their *own* sentencing practices. The absence of feedback to judges about their own performance was apparent in the study by Ashworth and colleagues who found that judges had somewhat imperfect knowledge of their own sentencing practices. Thus, one judge believed that he had reduced his sentences for certain categories of crime over the previous five years. However, the analysis of his decisions carried out by the research team did not bear this out. In other cases, where a judge claimed that he had passed a particularly lenient sentence, he had not in fact done so when the sentence was compared with his own previous practice.

The judges concerned were surprised and fascinated when their own sentencing profiles were presented to them. The researchers suggest that the reason judges were unaware of their own sentencing practices is that they have no fixed starting points from which to make reductions for mitigating factors. It is more likely that the lack of feedback hinders awareness of their own and other sentencers' practices.

Sentencers themselves have expressed a wish for more feedback on the outcome of sentences they award. Judge Cooke (1987) for example, stresses that he would greatly value much more feedback, but is constrained from asking for it because of the work for others entailed. He suggests that a system might be set up whereby a sample of cases from each sentencer is routinely followed through, and the outcomes conveyed to the sentencer. This, he suggests, would be especially valuable where a 'risky' sentence is concerned, such as trying to break the circle by not sending a recidivist back to prison.

THE SENTENCER IN CONTEXT

So far I have been concentrating on the sentencer as an individual engaged in a complex task, rather than as a character in a process involving many people. I have said that for sentencing to be carried out, structures and hypotheses must be brought to bear on the available information, but I have not said where these structures and hypotheses come from (beyond rather vaguely attributing them to 'experience'), nor what their content is likely to be. To understand sentencing it is necessary to see the sentencer in context.

A judge or magistrate must work within a very complicated and often ambiguous framework of law, policy and practice, with a combination of administrative, moral and utilitarian goals and constraints. Sentencing can be an emotive topic. Sentencers may bear the brunt of public scrutiny and criticism, especially when sentencing such crimes as rape. The process of developing sentencing skills could be seen as part of a process of socialization, or learning the role of a judge or magistrate and how things are done in practice as well as theory. Disparity in sentencing is perceived as more of a problem between *courts* than between *individual sentencers* within a court, suggesting that learning 'how it is done here' is of some importance. This is not to say that once socialized a sentencer is ossified. Feedback, guidance, administrative changes, policy changes, and so on, as well as personal experiences, may continually modify the categorizations and rules used to arrive at a decision: but a tendency to inertia can be expected.

Factors related to sentences imposed

A great many studies, largely sociological in approach, have been conducted looking at the relationship between characteristics of cases and the sentence imposed, which give some indication of the factors that may play a part. But very few studies have looked at the configurations, or recurring patterns of factors that might be used by sentencers to pigeon-hole cases. We are left with rather long lists of discrete factors, with little suggestion as to how these fall into patterns. One review of 140 sentencing studies identified 26 different factors reported to influence sentencing, including the charge, criminal record and various characteristics of the defendant, victim, and sentencer, such as age, sex and social background. Of these 26, 15 could be classified as not legitimately connected with sentence – for example, the age, sex, religion and social background of the sentencer; the race, socio-economic status and attractiveness of the offender; and the race of the victim. More recent studies are reported in Pennington and Lloyd-Bostock (1987). However, the evidence is often inconclusive or inconsistent from one study to the next.

Gravity of the offence

One reliable and rather obvious finding is that sentence relates to the gravity of the offence; but this only pushes the question back a step. How is gravity of offence decided? And how exactly does this relate to sentence?

Even though the concept of 'gravity', or 'seriousness', is rather loose, people, including judges and magistrates, are able to make judgements of the relative severity of offences, and these rankings are in remarkably close agreement across cultures, social classes and time, running from such offences as murder and armed robbery at one extreme to avoiding paying a bus fare and disturbing the neighbourhood at the other. The central components of gravity seem to be the amount of loss, damage and injury caused. Fitzmaurice and Pease suggest that the prevalence of the offence may also directly affect judged gravity in so far as 'gravity' includes in its meaning 'size of the social problem'.

These components do not, however, combine in a simple additive way. A number of researchers have looked for the arithmetic underlying how elements are combined; how the gravity of one offence is compared with another; and how gravity translates into sentence. Fitzmaurice and Pease, who are particularly interested in the arithmetic of sentencing, review several such studies. In one study each of five types of crime (burglary, cheque fraud, robbery, theft and rape) was linked to 10 points on a range of monetary loss, from $5 to $10,000. They found that the amount of money stolen did not simply add on a fixed degree of gravity per dollar. For example the amount of money stolen had very little effect on the judged seriousness of the rape; a slight effect in the robbery case; and the maximum effect in cheque fraud.

Other studies of policemen suggested that ratings of seriousness assigned to crimes do not combine in a straightforward way. If a policeman scores the value of preventing one particular crime as 30, and another as 10, then it should follow that he will value equally preventing one crime of the first type or three of the second type. However, this is not what happened. Typically, the subjects in this research expressed a preference for preventing one of the first type of crime rather than four (or more) of the second. This occurred even though according to their instructions on how to do the ratings, the subjects were being inconsistent. These particular studies concerned prevention and detection of crime rather than seriousness, but the judgements the policemen made seemed very similar to seriousness judgements.

Where separate offences are concerned, gravity is still not additive. Committing two identical offences is not judged to be twice as serious as committing only one of them. As Fitzmaurice and Pease point out, this is consistent with the practice of the Court of Appeal in reducing sentences composed of a series of consecutive prison terms. Even though each term taken on its own is judged to be correct, the aggregate can be judged excessive. As Fitzmaurice and Pease conclude, '"offence gravity" is not a variable on which one can sensibly do sums'.

As well as looking at offence gravity in itself, they also explore the possibility of representing the relationship between gravity of offence, sentence severity and sentence length in numerical terms. Custodial sentences, of course, traditionally go up in steps (three months, six months, etc) which get larger as the sentences get longer. Fines also go up in steps – but on a decimal rather than a duodecimal system. These oddities add to the complexities of relating sentence to gravity. If one assumes a retributive goal of sentencing, then sentence severity can be expected to increase as gravity of offence increases, and clearly a longer sentence is more severe than a shorter one. But the relationship between seriousness and length of sentence is not necessarily linear; and moreover, Fitzmaurice found that the way they related differed between two Crown Court judges she studied. For one, doubling sentence length less than doubled its severity; while for the other, an increase in length corresponded to an identical increase in severity. Where the relationship between offence seriousness and sentence length is concerned, results from three judges she studied (and also a student sample) showed that doubling of sentence length requires more than a doubling of offence seriousness.

Up to a point sentencers' decision making is structured and anchored by common policies, established practice, tariffs and guidelines, and to some degree, shared goals. But these goals embody dilemmas; and guidance, policy and practice leave a great deal unclear. It is hardly surprising that disparity is perceived to be a problem. Consistency in sentencing requires that sentencers agree on the seriousness of the type of crime; on the gravity of the particular offence and in their personal notions of the aims of sentencing and how these may be justly achieved. Very different sentences are sometimes given by magistrates in simulated sentencing exercises in the name of the same penal aim. Thus, in one simulated case, 70 magistrates, in order to deter the defendant, either bound him over to keep the peace, or gave him a conditional discharge or fined him up to £100. Eighteen magistrates gave him a custodial sentence in the name of the same aim.

Prior record

Besides offence seriousness, the other major determinant of sentencing is prior record. This, it seems, influences sentence directly rather than simply by making the offence more grave.

Prior record provides information on how set the offender is on a criminal career. This may lead to a moral judgement that the individual is more (or less) wicked, and hence deserving of a more (or less) severe sentence. It might also be seen as one dimension of the concept of responsibility. Bernard Weiner in 1979 proposed that the psychological meaning of causal responsibility is an intersection of three dimensions:

- whether the cause is seen as internal (within the person) or external (in the person's environment or other people);
- whether the cause is seen as stable, continuing over time; and
- whether the cause is seen as under the individual's control.

Thus where sentencing is concerned, a man who has a previous record (stable cause) and who plans and carries out a theft (controllable and internal) would be seen as more responsible than a man of previous good character (unstable cause) who carries out a similar theft while suffering from depression (internal uncontrollable and unstable cause), or led on by others (partly external). Bizarre and dangerous behaviour implies uncontrollable, internal causes.

The model, sometimes called the *attribution model*, provides a framework for conceptualizing the ways in which many of the factors commonly regarded as 'mitigating' or 'aggravating' operate, and for generating hypotheses about the relative severity of sentence to be expected for different combinations of factors. Variations of it have been applied successfully to studying parole decisions as well as sentencing.

Brian Ewart and Donald Pennington (1987) point out that classification according to this model logically relates to different sentencing goals. A stable controllable internal cause, which would be associated with an incorrigible offender, might relate to retributive goals; while causes perceived to be unstable or out of the offender's control might give rise to rehabilitative goals. This was indeed what they found in a sample drawn from the police and social services. Interestingly, in their observational study of Crown Courts they found that lenient sentences were accompanied by much more justification than severe ones – an average of 2.7 reasons per offender as compared with one reason. (Severity and leniency were determined by obtaining the views of court personnel, usually defence counsel or the court probation officer.) They suggest that giving reasons for sentence is serving a social function here, and that, in an atmosphere of retributivism, sentences that are lenient in retributive terms and that may imply a rehabilitative approach, need to be accounted for more fully.

Characteristics of the sentencer

The source of disparities in sentencing has sometimes been sought not in the parameters and definition of the task, but rather in the personal characteristics of judges – even the state of their digestion. John Hogarth (1971) writes '...we can explain more about sentencing by knowing a few things about the judge than by knowing a great deal about the facts of the case'.

For obvious reasons, studies of the personalities of judges are somewhat thin on the ground. There are a few in-depth studies of US judges but these tell us rather little about how individual judges vary in their sentencing practices. Forty years ago someone actually psychoanalysed three judges. One he found to be a compulsive personality, lacking in warmth, and preoccupied with detail. He tended to be very severe in his sentencing, imposing high fines and long prison terms. The second was relaxed, easy-going, and sensitive to others, and was viewed as much more benevolent and less severe. The third was very ambitious, demanded deference and had a mercurial temper. He tended to be soft on youthful offenders and the aged, and severe with the middle-aged.

Another more recent study, developed a typology of trial judges, on the basis of observations of nine judges in one court. The researchers identified six types: an intellectual scholar and a 'routineer hack' were the workhorses of the court; two 'political adventurer-careerists' saw the bench as a stepping stone to other office; two 'judicial pensioners' had to all intents and purposes retired; a 'hatchet man' was a former district attorney still with close links with the prosecutor's office, whose image was of a swift dispenser of justice; and a 'tyrant showboat-benevolent despot', who was a sadistic exhibitionist whose severity depended on his mood (Smith and Blumberg, 1967).

These studies tell us little of substance. But the existence of differences in the sentencing propensities of different judges in the UK is confirmed by research on the listing of cases. Clerks responsible for the listing of cases to appear before different judges quite clearly do this partly with reference to their knowledge of how different judges sentence particular sorts of cases. Austin Lovegrove (1984) has set out the relevant judicial characteristics that emerged from his interviews with 13 clerks and listing officers at nine English Crown Court centres. These included competence in a range of skills, as well as attitudes to particular sorts of cases, willingness to impose severe sentences, and other personal characteristics. Of course, the clerks could be mistaken in believing that such consistent differences exist, but it is unlikely that these are wholly illusory. Barristers, too, clearly believe judges vary in the attitude they are likely to take, and may deviously attempt to avoid a particular judge, perhaps by introducing delay. There is a story that, until the display board was made inaccessible behind glass, cards allocating cases to particular judges at the Old Bailey would mysteriously move from one slot to another.

'Framing' of the information received by sentencers

What is missing from Hogarth's statement about the effects of the judge as compared with the facts of the case, quoted above, is the many other constraints, influences, and dilemmas surrounding sentencing, which are neither 'facts of the case' nor idiosyncrasies of the sentencer. Sentencers necessarily rely heavily on others in the criminal justice process for the information on which they base their decisions. Judges and magistrates are not working from raw material, but from material that has already undergone a considerable amount of processing, filtering, structuring, preparation and rehearsing. Some criminologists have suggested that they in fact play quite a secondary role in sentencing. Joanna

Shapland in a chapter called 'Who controls sentencing?' (1987) has set out some of the various sources of information available to sentencers, and the ways in which these sources are controlled by others, and constrained by court processes. Keith Hawkins (1987) has emphasized the importance of the way in which 'facts' are described. The same behaviour may for example be described as showing remorse or as being insincere or manipulative. These differences serve to frame the decision for the decision maker. Konecni and Ebbesen go much further, and see judges' sentencing decisions as rhetorical rubber-stamping exercises (see p. 66).

Psychiatric reports

A beautiful example of the way in which bias can be built in to the information available to sentencers comes from the study of psychiatric reports to the courts by Hilary Allen (1987). Allen painstakingly analysed 260 psychiatric reports, and found quite different patterns of sentencing recommendations for men and women, for very similar offences including co-offenders. Women were in general portrayed in passive terms. The crime was not so much something they had done and were responsible for, as something that had happened to them, and for which they deserved sympathy, counselling, probation or therapy rather than punishment. In contrast, men, even where mental illness, or mental handicap was acknowledged, were none the less portrayed as active agents, responsible for their actions, and fit for any disposal the court might decide on, including prison. Even if treatment seemed appropriate, this was more likely to be in a secure setting.

For example, in one case Allen quotes, a woman had stabbed her boyfriend to death in the course of an argument over money. The psychiatric report portrays the woman as small, mild and no danger to anyone, a good mother, a loyal and faithful partner despite having been persistently abused, and as suffering anguish and psychological scars as a result of the 'events of the night in question'. Her own violence is glossed over. Although she knifed her boyfriend through the heart, the report improbably suggests that Mary acted without any intent to cause him physical harm. The just and appropriate disposal, it is suggested, is a programme of social rehabilitation, practical and probationary support, and psychotherapy – a proposal that was accepted by the court.

In contrast, Allen quotes a case of a man convicted of arson. As a child he had suffered brain damage that had resulted in low intelligence, epilepsy, and poor control over his behaviour. He had frequently been admitted to hospital with depression and was currently diagnosed as suffering from depression. These clinical details are discussed at length in the report, but not in such a way as to excuse the offence in any way. Allen quotes from the report:

> No evidence of any pyschiatric disorder which would interfere with his judgement or responsibility was discovered. He does have the personality disorder with some temporal lobe activity, but he was told this in the past, and knows that he is liable to impulsive behaviour when the stress factors in his life become too high. . . . I am unable to assist the court with any specific psychiatric recommendations. He is mentally and physically fit for whatever course the Court should wish to take.

The same qualities of immaturity, dependence, etc., that in women provide the basis for a supportive and therapeutic recommendation, are in men likely to be seen as signs merely of inadequacy. Thus in one arson case, a man was described in the psychiatric report as a 'manipulative and childish individual', who misses his wife badly but is behaving 'like a spoilt child trying to regain something' and for whom probation would reinforce his dependency. 'He has to learn to take responsibility for his own actions.' No recommendation of treatment was made, and the man received a seven-year prison sentence.

Women were rarely regarded as dangerous, and far more likely to be regarded as treatable. Whereas the commonest medical recommendation and action for female killers diagnosed as disordered was probationary supervision (even if this meant returning a woman to live with family members she had previously attempted to kill), in male homicide cases this disposal was *never* suggested or offered.

In another example, the report on a woman with an extremely violent history begins with what Allen calls a 'catalogue of nastiness' – a dozen or more episodes of assaults and woundings including attacks on children. However, when the report comes to its conclusions the violence seems to be forgotten. The woman is described not as dangerous, but as insecure, deprived, and lonely. The court accepted a recommendation for psychiatric treatment on probation. Males with a history of violent crime; on the other hand, are typically seen only as suitable for treatment in secure custodial settings, if at all. These remarkable differences cannot, Allen concludes, be accounted for by actual differences in the level of psychopathology among male and female offenders, nor their therapeutic needs.

Allen puts forward a convincing analysis of the logic of these reports and their recommendations, which refers both to the different assumptions that medical personnel bring to the assessment of men and women, and to the various judicial, clinical and institutional criteria that influence the psychiatric recommendation made. The net result is that women are at a very marked advantage in the competition for treatment resources. The information the sentencer receives through these reports has already been processed in such a way as to frame the sentencing decision in a certain way; and of course, the recommendation carries the weight of medical expertise.

There is a multitude of similar possible ways in which the information and advice reaching the sentencer is designed and influenced by witnesses, the police, prosecutors and defence, probation officers and others, and by the interactions amongst these people. Sentencers themselves, of course, often sit in groups, and some research has been done on the dynamics of joint decisions. There is some evidence, for example, that the result is not an averaging out of the different positions towards a compromise, but instead a tendency toward extremes. Joint deliberation should, however, serve to iron out idiosyncrasies in sentencing. Sentencers are also increasingly bombarded with guidance and training, new statutory provisions, and rather vaguer pressure to be consistent, keep down the prison population, and in various ways take account of local resources and constraints.

Options and resources

One factor brought out by Allen in the study discussed above is that of limits on the availability of different options, and the ways in which legal provisions such as section 37 of the Mental Health Act 1983, and section 3 of Powers of the Criminal Courts Act 1973 operate. As she shows, it can make all the difference to an offender's fate whether or not he or she is defined as a suitable case, and whether 'appropriate' treatment is available.

Suzanne Dell, in her study of sentencing in cases of 'diminished responsibility' homicide found that the prospects of release differed greatly depending on whether the original disposal was a special hospital or a prison (Dell, 1983). As in Allen's study, these differences could not be wholly explained with reference to the crime concerned, nor the psychopathology of the offender. Release from special hospitals could occur quite soon. One fifth of her sample was out in three years, and half after seven years. The main consideration was the safety of the public; consideration of tariff did not enter the decision. In contrast, release from prison centrally incorporated a strong notion of tariff. Until 1973, the case for release would normally not even be considered until seven years had been served. Under the more recent (but since modified) review procedure, a decision was taken after about three or four years as to when a lifer's first parole review should take place. In about half the cases no date was set, and in the other half it was usually set for a time when the prisoner would have served eight to ten years.

Dell cites instances of cases that could equally have become either lifers in prison or section 65 cases in a special hospital depending on such chance events as whether a bed was available in the special hospital, and where the stark contrast in time served before release seems arbitrary and unfair. In one example, a sex offender's admission to Broadmoor (the hospital for mentally disordered offenders) was not originally recommended. He was on the brink of a life sentence, when it transpired that a bed in Broadmoor would be offered. A further medical report was therefore made, and the man was made the subject of a hospital order. Another case concerned a youth with a blameless record who stabbed a workmate. Psychiatric opinion was divided, but a Broadmoor bed was made available and a section 65 order made on the grounds of psychopathic disorder. Within three-and-a-half years he was back with his family.

The fate of another youth contrasts greatly with this. He also had a blameless record, but lost control and killed a girl who was said to have provoked him. Although the prison medical officer regarded the outburst as amounting to abnormality of mind within the meaning of section 2 of the Homicide Act 1957, he did not recommend a hospital order. Dell quotes the judge, in imposing a life sentence, as follows: 'Life imprisonment does not necessarily mean imprisonment for very many years. As soon as the doctors are satisfied that it is safe to release you to go back to your family you will go back.' The case was not reviewed for release for years, and it was seven years before he went out. Dell comments: 'In spite of the judge's words, which made it clear that considerations of tariff were not in his mind when he imposed the sentence, the possibility of release was not looked at until the usual tariff had been served'.

The sentencer in context: a summary

Judges and magistrates' sentencing decisions must therefore be seen in context. Their options are constrained, their intentions may be thwarted, and they rely greatly on others' interpretations and recommendations. It is to be hoped that future research will not only concentrate on the psychology of the sentencer but also pay attention to the wider context of sentencing, the individual and group psychology of other characters in the process, and the sources, forms and sequences of information sentencers are receiving. Hilary Allen's study of psychiatric reports illustrates how illuminating and important such research could be.

Finally, I have concentrated in this chapter on the psychology of how sentencing decisions are taken. I have not asked the question 'What do we know about the effects and effectiveness of different sentences, treatments and regimes for offenders?' The answer to this further question is, unfortunately, not encouraging, but the picture is not totally bleak. There are, for instance, some interesting new developments involving psychologists in treatment programmes for inveterate car thieves. However, the effectiveness of sentences is beyond the scope of this book. The two questions are obviously linked. One major factor in sentencing decisions must surely be the perceived effectiveness (or otherwise) of sentences. But from a psychological point of view they are quite different. The first raises questions about decision-making processes, while the second is a question about how to change behaviour.

In conclusion . . .

Sentencing is a complex and ill-structured task, partly moral and partly instrumental, without clear criteria for correct solutions. As skill at sentencing develops through experience the decision becomes more automatic. New cases are more likely to be treated as falling into types and categories the sentencer has seen before. There are drawbacks as well as advantages in more automatic, skill-based decision making. Cases may too readily be slotted into the sentencer's repertoire of 'typical cases'. Biases may arise from cognitive strategies used to reduce the amount of information processing required. Apparent idiosyncracies and inconsistencies result from the rational strategies sentencers use to cope with the complexities and ambiguities of sentencing. Judges and magistrates should not be considered in isolation but in the context of their experience; the usual practice of the particular court; the roles of others in the sentencing process; and the need to rely on information already framed towards someone else's conclusion.

Research into sentencing has been impeded by difficulties in obtaining the necessary permissions and access. Encouraging further research and making the results available to researchers would be valuable in itself. Insight into how such a task is accomplished can make sentencers and others aware of the potential dangers and weaknesses in the process. Sentencers who are aware that they tend to classify cases as 'typical' of a class are more likely to guard against the dangers of doing so too readily. There is little psychologists can do to resolve the moral and administrative dilemmas facing sentencers, but the complexity of the information processing demanded might be reduced by changing the sequence and form in which information about a case is presented to sentencers. Further research is needed to explore whether, for example, some information would be easier to use and evaluate if presented in a standardized written format.

The value of providing feedback on the outcomes of sentences awarded emerges repeatedly from both the psychological literature and the views of the sentencers themselves. (This of course assumes a utilitarian approach to at least some degree.) The plea for more feedback is part of a wider plea by both sentencers and researchers for more information to be provided for sentencers and for a clearer structure to sentencing decisions.

References

Allen, H. (1987) The logic of gender in psychiatric reports to the courts. In D.C. Pennington and S.M.A. Lloyd-Bostock (ed.) *The Psychology of Sentencing: Approaches to consistency and disparity*. Oxford: Centre for Socio-Legal Studies.

Ashworth, A., Genders, E., Mansfield, G., Peay, J. and Player, E. (1984) *Sentencing in the Crown Court*. Occasional Paper No. 10, Centre for Criminological Research, University of Oxford.

Broadbent, D.E. (1984) 'The Psychology of Risk'. *Wolfson College Lecture Series on Risk: Man Made Hazards to Man*.

Cooke, Judge R.K. (1987) The practical problems of the sentencer. In D.C. Pennington and S.M.A. Lloyd-Bostock (ed.) *The Psychology of Sentencing: Approaches to consistency and disparity*. Oxford: Centre for Socio-Legal Studies.

Dell, S (1983) The detention of diminished responsibility homicide offenders. *British Journal of Criminology, 23, 1*, 50–60.

Ewart, B. and Pennington, D.C. (1987) An attributional approach to explaining sentencing disparity. In D.C. Pennington and S.M.A. Lloyd-Bostock (ed) *The Psychology of Sentencing: Approaches to consistency and disparity*. Oxford: Centre for Socio-Legal Studies.

*Fitzmaurice, C. and Pease, K. (1986) *The Psychology of Judicial Sentencing*. Manchester: Manchester University Press.

Frank, J. (1930) *Law and the Modern Mind*. Reprinted 1970, Gloucester, Massachusetts: Peter Smith.

Hawkins, K.O. (1987) *Discretion in Making Legal Decisions, Washington and Lee Law Review 43, 4* (whole issue).

Hogarth, J. (1971) *Sentencing as a Human Process*: Toronto: University of Toronto Press.

Konecni, V.J. and Ebbesen, E.E. (1982) *The Criminal Justice System: A Social Psychological Analysis*. San Francisco: W.H. Freeman & Company.

Lawrence, J. and Homel, R. (1986) Sentencing in magistrates' courts: The magistrate as professional decision-maker. In I. Potas (ed.) *Sentencing in Australia: Policies, Issues and Reform.* Canberra: Australian Institute of Criminology.

Lovegrove, S.A. (1984) The listing of criminal cases in the crown court as an administrative discretion. *Criminal Law Review, December,* 738–744.

Nisbett, R.E. and Ross, L. (1980). *Human Inference: Strategies and Shortcomings of Social Judgment.* Englewood Cliffs, New Jersey: Prentice Hall Inc.

Nisbett, R.E. and Wilson, T.D. (1977) Telling more than we can know: Verbal reports on mental processes. *Psychological Review, 84.* 231–249.

Payne, J. W. (1980) Information processing theory: some concepts and methods applied to decision research. In T.S. Wallsten (ed.) *Cognitive Processes in Choice and Decision Behavior.* Hillsdale, New Jersey: Lawrence Erlbaum Associates.

*Pennington, D. C. and Lloyd-Bostock, S.M.A. (ed.) (1987) *The Psychology of Sentencing: Approaches to consistency and disparity.* Oxford: Centre for Socio-Legal Studies.

Shapland, J. (1987) Who controls sentencing? Influences on the sentencer. In D.C. Pennington and S.M.A. Lloyd-Bostock (ed.) (1987) *The Psychology of Sentencing: Approaches to consistency and disparity.* Oxford: Centre for Socio-Legal Studies.

Smith, A. and Blumberg, A. (1967) The problem of objectivity in judicial decision-making. *Social Forces 46,* 96–105.

Thomas, D.A. (1979) *Principles of Sentencing,* 2nd edn. London: Heinemann.

Weiner, B. (1979) A theory of motivation for some classroom experiences. *Journal of Educational Psychology, 71,* 3–25.

Wickens, C. D. (1984) *Engineering Psychology and Human Performance.* Columbus: A. Bell & Howell Company.

Further reading

Publications marked with an asterisk (*) above.

Chapter 5

Children and the Law

Children become involved in legal cases in a variety of roles: as witnesses, as offenders – even almost as a form of property in cases of custody after divorce, or adoption. In all these roles they are treated as psychologically (as well as physically) different from adults. Their perceived emotional needs, responses and interests as victims or in custody cases are to a large extent special to them as children. Their evidence as witnesses is expected to be especially unreliable, and their delinquent or criminal behaviour is understood and responded to in different terms.

The issues raised here go much wider than psychology. Conceptions of childhood in our society, the rights and responsibilities of adults towards children, and other social and moral questions are involved. Childhood is often seen as an important and precious time, during which the foundations are laid for a happy and stable adulthood. The discipline of psychology has influenced these perceptions to some extent, but it is also necessarily influenced *by* them. As in other fields of law and psychology, the topics investigated by psychologists are influenced by values and social norms. Questions asked about children are themselves bound up with perceptions of, for example, what we mean by a 'family' or what is regarded as a 'good' upbringing . These perceptions vary from one social group to another, and may change over time. A central problem for psychology is distinguishing say, what is general and perhaps biologically based in parent–child relationships, and what is a function of the society the parents and children happen to live in. There can be no doubt that a mother and a new-born infant respond to each other in ways that involve powerful biological factors. But to what extent is the relationship between a mother and her child crucial to a child's development?

Value judgements about how families and children ought to be treated by our society are especially difficult to disentangle from recommendations based on empirical research. It is also an emotive area. It is easy to arouse adults' feelings towards young children as innocent or vulnerable. But the treatment of legal cases involving children does raise quite distinct pyschological questions. What are the psychological effects of divorce on children and how may they be mitigated? What are the emotional effects on a child of becoming involved in a court case? Are the causes of delinquent behaviour qualitatively different at different ages? I shall consider the extent to which we have the answers to these questions.

CHILDREN AS WITNESSES

Public concern about the plight of abused children has brought to the fore concern about their experiences as witnesses. Children also appear in other sorts of cases – such as road traffic cases – but it is as the victims of sexual abuse that they have attracted most attention. As with so many aspects of the criminal and civil justice system, no one knows how often children actually appear as witnesses. What is known is that children who have been victims of abuse are sometimes subjected to the extremely unpleasant experience of appearing in a daunting courtroom in the presence of the accused, being disbelieved (or apparently disbelieved), being repeatedly interrogated about the events in question, and being attacked in cross-examination. The Division of Criminological and Legal Psychology of The British Psychological Society aptly entitled a conference on this topic in 1986 'The Child Witness: Do the Courts Abuse Children?' In one case, for example, a young child dived terrified under the clerk's table and refused to come out. The process of appearing in court has been described as 're-victimizing' the child.

A number of questions need to be separated here. The emotional effects of appearing in a court case are not necessarily related to the reliability of a child's testimony. The question of reliability further breaks down into questions about moral and intellectual development, recall and recognition by children as compared with adults, and the capacity of children to resist suggestion.

Emotional effects of involvement in a court case

Telling the story of abuse and the long-drawn-out process of prosecution are traumatic experiences for a child of any age. It is hardly surprising that studies have found that children are frightened, disturbed and sometimes feel betrayed. There are so many factors involved that it is not yet possible to reach firm conclusions about the effects of giving testimony in itself. Where the accused person is a member of the family, the child may be very frightened of breaking up the family – a fear that is well founded. These fears may account for much of the distress apparent in children who give evidence in such cases. Conversely, there are some indications that appearing in court can sometimes have positive psychological effects, by placing the child in a powerful role, instead of the role of the victim, and vindicating the child by publicly accepting the child's version of events. But for this to occur, the child needs to be properly prepared and supported.

Research under way in the United States by Gail Goodman is designed to tease out the main factors causing psychological distress to children who act as witnesses. Her research team has been contacting families at the point where the District Attorney (DA) is thinking of prosecuting in a case of child sexual abuse. (The initial request to participate in the study is made by the DA's office.) These cases then take different directions. Only a minority of the children end up testifying. Sometimes the defendant confesses. Sometimes defendants agree to plead guilty to a lesser charge. The children are assessed at various stages. To avoid interviewing the children more than necessary the assessment is done through parents and teachers who can say, for example, how often a child wets his bed, has nightmares, etc. The researchers also have information on the alleged incidents from the DA's office: what the allegations are, whether physical force was involved, the child's relationship to the accused, and so on. If the child attends the court, he or she is interviewed before and after testifying, and again three months later.

The researchers want to disentangle such factors as the children's initial emotional disturbance, the severity of the assault, and their relationship to the defendant, from the effects of the court appearance as such. To do this they have built up two groups: a 'court group' and a matching 'non-court group', who match the others on these other variables (severity of assault, etc.) but do not testify in court.

The study is not yet complete, but results so far show that, controlling for other factors, appearing in court does result in higher behavioural disturbance. The court group is more anxious, shows more psychosomatic symptoms and is more depressed. The children's degree of disturbance *before* any court appearance is related to the severity of the assault and the child's relationship to the accused person. The children were better adjusted when the parents were supportive and the child felt believed. The effects of attending court add to such effects. Interviews with the children showed that they had negative feelings about appearing in court. They felt scared and nervous, and wanted their parents to be with them. (Usually this was not possible because the parent would also be testifying.) They expressed anger and fear at the prospect of seeing the accused.

There can be little doubt that much could be done to lessen the ordeal of a court appearance for children. Much is indeed already being tried and the judicial system of England and Wales lags behind many others, including the Scottish system, in this respect. Judges sometimes do their best to shed some of the trappings of the court: wigs, gowns, high seats, and the like. The use of videotape in various ways can avoid the necessity for the child's physical presence in court. As well as reducing trauma, this probably allows the child to be a more competent witness, since anxiety interferes with memory. The video-link system, whereby a child can give evidence via a closed-circuit television, is a step in this direction. At the time of writing, it seems this will be introduced soon in Britain: it is already used in most states in the US.

But psychologists and some lawyers are urging that the more significant step should be taken of allowing videotape of an interview with a child to be presented as evidence in a later court case. Earlier statements have inherent value. They are obtained nearer to the events in question, and before the child has undergone repeated retelling and questioning that might make his or her memory less reliable (see Chapter 1). They also avoid continued 're-traumatization' of children, through repeated interviewing and possibly rehearsal for a dreaded court appearance. If such a system is to be introduced, techniques for conducting these interviews will be needed. Unfortunately here, as in other clinical settings, therapeutic and legal goals may be in conflict. A therapeutic interview may well emphasize drawing out the story in ways that are too suggestive to be acceptable for legal purposes.

The reliability of child witnesses

Legal barriers to children's evidence. This leads us to the question of the reliability of children's evidence. Many of the legal barriers to making things easier for child witnesses arise from the rules of evidence concerning children's statements. The rules about convicting on uncorroborated evidence single out children and those complaining of a sexual offence as categories of witness especially likely to be unreliable. At the time I write, in England and Wales conviction is not allowed on the basis of the unsworn and uncorroborated evidence of a child. Even where the child gives evidence on oath, a judge must warn the jury that it is 'dangerous' to convict on this basis. John Spencer, an academic lawyer who has taken a special interest in this topic, sets out the existing rules in detail and writes 'There is a widespread belief amongst lawyers . . . that children are unreliable, never less than when they testify about sexual assault' (1987). Moreover, what the child told its parents, doctor, the police, or others, about the incident, is usually inadmissible as evidence because it amounts to hearsay. One unsworn child cannot corroborate another. There is often no possibility in child abuse cases of corroboration that satisfies the various legal tests.

There has been considerable resistance to changing the rules. However, in October 1987 the Home Secretary announced that he would be proposing to parliament a radical change, lifting the bar to conviction on the unsworn, uncorroborated evidence of a child over five years of age. But how much protection of the accused is justified? Are children specially unreliable as witnesses?

Lying and the oath. The first issue is whether children are liable to lie. An important distinction has been made between a child's sworn and unsworn testimony. The ability to understand the nature of the oath certainly develops with age; but to what extent does the ability to grasp moral concepts relate to the accuracy of a child's testimony?

Psychology has shown developmental trends in the *reasons* people give to justify behaviour. As children get older, their reasons become increasingly morally sophisticated and show increased grasp of moral concepts. However, no age-trends in *honesty* have been found. It would seem, therefore, that understanding the nature of the oath and the difference between truth and lies is not at all the same as being less likely to lie. This understanding may tell us about the child's intellectual development, but it is not likely to tell us much about his or her propensity in general to tell the truth.

This leaves the question of whether taking the oath makes a child more likely to tell the truth on this particular occasion. There is no evidence that the oath is special in this respect. It is possible that sometimes it serves to emphasize the importance of telling the truth to the court or induces fear of the consequences of lying on this occasion. But the same result may be produced in other ways. Understanding the nature of the oath does not deserve the prominence it has had in decisions as to the admissibility of a child's evidence.

Children's memories. The second issue is whether a child intending to tell the truth is less capable than an adult of doing so accurately. Research is continuing on this point, and it is not yet possible to give clear-cut answers. It seems that young children do differ from adults in the way they remember and recall events, but that these differences do not necessarily undermine the accuracy of their evidence. Indeed, within their own familiar world, they can do much better than adults in some memory tasks.

The distinction between recall and recognition is important. Young children have consistently been found to volunteer less information when asked to recall and freely describe an incident. Spontaneous accounts became steadily fuller with age. However, what younger children do produce has sometimes been found to be *more* correct than the reports of older children. When a different measure is used, involving recognition rather than spontaneous recall, there is little difference between, say, a five year old and a ten year old.

Cues and prompts are disproportionately effective with younger as compared with older children. Graham Davies and Rhona Flin (1988) suggest that younger children are less competent at retrieving information systematically from memory. If young children are prompted or provided with cues to help them remember, they are able to produce a great deal more information. In one study the researchers found they could completely iron out differences between young children, older children and adults by careful use of questions.

As well as problems in retrieving information, young children are handicapped by their limited experiences and understanding. Understanding and memory are very closely linked. A young child obviously understands less than an adult. But sometimes a young child can outperform older children and adults, because they know more about the subject, or because it holds special interest for them.

Children's suggestibility. A third factor that might make children less reliable is simply their status as children being interviewed by an adult. It is important for adults to establish rapport if a child is to give a coherent account. In addition, some of the social pressures to produce 'helpful' evidence discussed in Chapter 1 may be more powerful in their effect upon children. For example, if a great big adult has gone to the trouble to lay out a set of photographs, he or she must have a good reason, and the child is likely to pick out somebody. The suggestibility of children has led to concern over the use of 'anatomically correct dolls' as an aid to interviews with children who may have been sexually abused. Sometimes, when a child is having difficulty telling his or her story, the interviewer may guide the child with quite leading suggestions. Even the simple existence of genitalia on the dolls may attract the child's attention and produce play that involves these interesting extras not usually found on dolls. The dolls, and sometimes a leading style of interviewing, have been very successful from a therapeutic perspective. Children have been able to express themselves in ways they had not previously been able to do. But there may be problems for any future legal case when early interviews, carried out for therapeutic purposes, have been suggestive. Work is in progress evaluating the use of anatomically correct dolls, and studying the reactions to them of non-abused children.

In several studies, however, children have been shown to be extremely resistant to suggestion. Like adults, children tend to be suggestible concerning minor details (see Chapter 1). But when it comes to the central thread of events, they are as resistant to suggestion as adults. In one interesting study by Gail Goodman and colleagues (1988), children were watched and filmed attending a clinic for inoculations. This is a particularly apt setting, since it involves the children in an unpleasant and stressful physical experience that can be compared in many respects with a sexual assault. She found that the children were very accurate about what had happened. They were somewhat poor at identifying the nurse from photographs – but here they did no worse than their parents. In another study, a game with clowns and photographers was arranged to mimic a pornographic photographing session. Here again the children were very accurate about all central details – such as exactly what clothes the clown had asked them to remove. When they made errors, these were errors of omission (for example, a girl saying that she was not touched at all when in fact the clown had touched her) rather than errors in the direction that might lead to false accusations.

Children as witnesses: summary and conclusions

There is growing research evidence that in the right circumstances children can be as reliable as witnesses as are adults. There is also plenty of anecdotal evidence to support this. Children as young as two and three years old have been able to provide remarkably accurate accounts and make accurate identifications. Extra care is needed to question children skilfully. But the inherent unreliability of children as witnesses does seem to have been exaggerated.

Present rules of procedure and evidence therefore cause needless problems for the child witness and err on the side of protecting the accused to an unnecessary degree. The rules in England and Wales on corroboration of a child's evidence are not supported by psychological research. The hearsay rules are extremely restricting in cases of child abuse. The question of what changes and reforms are called for is not straightforward. More work needs to be done on many topics, including the interviewing of children. But it seems obvious that a child victim should be spared a court appearance where possible, and provided with every support and preparation where this is unavoidable. Both video-link and videotaped interviews are promising approaches to achieving this.

CHILDREN AND DIVORCE

The dramatic rise in the divorce rate, together with legislative changes and debate in several countries, have given rise to a series of studies of the effects of divorce on children, and of ways of helping to decide on the best custody arrangements. There are two levels at which psychologists (and other social scientists) have approached this question. The first is to attempt to evaluate different beliefs and rules of thumb about the effects of divorce, or the best custody and access arrangements. For example, should there be a presumption in favour of giving custody to the mother? Is joint custody in general desirable? The second is through involvement at a more individual level, in helping to decide custody in a particular case. This involves psychologists acting as experts (see Chapter 7).

There is no doubt that conflict between parents, separation and divorce cause pain to children. While this is no new discovery, the degree and duration of many children's distress at the breakup of their parents' marriage has probably been underestimated. Recent research has begun to document how extensive these effects are and to look at patterns and causes for them. While acute unhappiness at the time of separation is virtually universal, long-term effects are also frequent and perhaps of more concern. Children who are below school age at the time of their parents' divorce, especially boys, seem to be more seriously affected in the long term than older children. However, emotional and behavioural problems are found in children of divorce of all ages.

Initial reactions

A study in California by Judith Wallerstein and Joan Kelly showed effects that are fairly typical. Their book *Surviving the Breakup* makes vivid and depressing reading. They studied a sample of 60 families from the time of separation to five years afterwards. There were 131 children ranging in age from three to 18. In all but one family the children remained with the mother after separation. The book could profitably be read by any parents considering divorce. The first year or two after separation was a time of considerable disorganization, disruption and change for parents and children alike. Other studies have confirmed that children's lives generally go through a very disrupted and unpredictable period, during which the parents are frequently depressed. The children's initial responses to the breakup can therefore be seen as responses not just to the change in the composition of the family, but to the whole drama precipitated by the parents' decision to separate. The youngest group of nursery-age children (up to the age of five) were confused and frightened by the separation. They became sad, clingy and whiney, seeking a great deal of physical contact and attention from adults, including strange adults. They might regress in toilet training, or their development might be delayed for a while in other ways. Children from around the age of five or six reacted similarly, but were better able to understand what was happening, and did not blame themselves as the very young ones sometimes did. School-age children were more able to express their feelings of intense sadness, anger, and rejection. There was an overwhelming opposition to the divorce, and desire for the reconciliation of their parents. Older pre-adolescent children might feel ashamed and morally outraged by their parents' behaviour. They frequently felt lonely and rejected. Adolescents were most openly upset by the separation, reacting with profound grief, and expressing strong feelings of anger, shame, sadness and embarrassment.

Although these findings relate to a somewhat unrepresentative Californian sample, they are very much in accordance with other studies. Another area where disruption is often apparent is school. This is brought out in Mavis Hetherington's research (1981). Relationships at school, both with peers and teachers, often suffer. Schools and nurseries usually notice a deterioration in the child's behaviour, concentration and mood, and increased absences from school are common. (Parents often fail to inform schools, and this can add to the difficulties for the child.)

An additional factor emphasized by Ann Mitchell in her book *Children in the Middle* (1985) (based on a study in Edinburgh) was the need the children felt to have things explained, and to be kept informed. Separating couples, it seems, are often so caught up in their own problems that they are unable to give attention to their children's. The separation was often not explained at all to children in Ann Mitchell's sample and sometimes came as a bolt from the blue. In one case, the first a little girl knew of the separation was when she was on her way home from Brownies one day and saw her mother at the bus stop with a suitcase. In another case a boy came home from school at lunch time to find no one in the house. He found his mother next door; she told him his father had left and sent him out to play. He recalled (seven years later) that his mother had been in tears and was being comforted by the other woman, but no one offered to comfort him.

Longer-term effects

However traumatic and stressful the time of separation may be, the longer-term outcome may be thought to be better for the children than remaining in a conflict-ridden marriage. How children fare in the years after the separation varies greatly. In most children the initial upset and unhappiness recede over the first year or two, but there are studies showing that effects may persist throughout childhood, especially if the divorce occurred before the age of five. It is common for children to continue to wish for their parents' reunion for many years, sometimes into adulthood, even though they know that this is unrealistic. In the Wallerstein and Kelly study 30 per cent of the children were still very unhappy and disapproving of the divorce at the five-year follow-up. The children who remained very unhappy fell into four groups: those (the most numerous) whose fathers had been erratic and inconstant in their interest in the child; those whose parents continued to fight intensely and used the children as messengers of hostility; those whose relationship with the custodial parent was poor because of that parent's own stress; and those who had been left in the care of a psychiatrically-disturbed mother.

A further follow-up after ten years has recently been carried out and found that the worst outcome for the children was associated with the parents' continuing hostility (often combined with a poor or non-existent relationship with the non-custodial parent). It is clear from the Wallerstein and Kelly research as well as other work that children are sometimes subject to very considerable stress after divorce as a result of being drawn into the parents' continued fighting and because of their parents' psychiatric problems. Such children continue to suffer in comparison with other children of divorce, and their suffering may even increase rather than abate. It is clearly damaging to children when they are themselves drawn into intense conflicts. But if this can be avoided the fact that their parents are not in a positive relationship can be of less importance to them than maintaining contact with both parents. The value to a child of maintaining a good relationship with the non-custodial parent may outweigh in the long run a good deal of increased awareness of hostile feelings between the parents.

Custody and access

This last factor – the continuing relationship with the non-custodial parent – is of course of particular significance where custody and access decisions are concerned. Access of one weekend in two has been widely accepted as reasonable, without any empirical base. In Wallerstein and Kelly's research, two thirds of the children had contact with their father at a level usually defined as 'reasonable visitation', but only 20 per cent of these children were at all satisfied with the visiting situation. Some (but not all) non-custodial fathers are more likely to continue maintenance payments if they see the child on a regular basis.

The quality as well as the frequency of visits is important. The negative effects of divorce on children can be greatly mitigated where the non-custodial parent (usually the father) is committed to the relationship with his children and is prepared to work at maintaining contact. Contact by letter or telephone can be very important.

Another strong argument for maintaining a relationship with the non-custodial parent is that this allows continuing links with the wider kinship group of grandparents, cousins, aunts. Sometimes children of divorce lose not only one parent, but also half their relations.

There is growing support for the belief that custody as well as access arrangements should encourage the continued role of both parents after divorce. In the US in particular, an increasing number of parents are arranging a much more equal division of their child's time between them, rather than the traditional pattern of living with one parent, plus visits to or from the other every two weeks or so. Living alternate weeks or fortnights with each parent has proved very successful in some cases. It is obviously an enormous advantage if the parents live close enough for the child to attend the same school and keep up the same social network from each home. In some cases, to avoid disrupting the children's schooling and social lives, children remain living in the same house while their parents take it in turns to live with them. A variety of other arrangements have been tried, and there is accumulating evidence that for some children they can be successful. Children do not necessarily seem to have great difficulty in relating to two parents who are not in positive contact nor in adapting to two different households with differing patterns of life, rules, and values.

However, a careful evaluation of these kinds of arrangements is needed. Joint physical custody is not always going to be the best solution. Some of the more extreme versions, involving six months in California and six months in New York, are much more questionable than shorter periods spent with parents living in the same area. Depending on the particular child, joint physical custody, where care of the child is shared, may be frightening or disconcerting to the child. Lenore Weitzman in her book *The Divorce Revolution* (1985) quotes (from a study by Jessica Pearson and Nancy Thoeness) the case of a nine-year-old boy who lived one month with his mother and then one month with his father, and who was having noticeable difficulty coping with the arrangement. He felt his life was in disarray, was preoccupied about loss and keeping track of things, and was not doing well at school. When interviewed he volunteered that the big problem with joint custody is that 'you have to remember where the spoons are' – a comment which the researchers say reflected all his other worries and sense of instability. However, it would be unfortunate if cases where joint custody does not work well were used to argue against its use in all cases.

Weitzman (and others) have also questioned whether custody arrangements can be an effective way of ensuring the child maintains a relationship with the non-custodial parent. As she points out, those couples in the Wallerstein and Kelly study who were co-operating over access and keeping up a relationship with the children were those who were both able and willing to do so. But is the outcome still positive for children when this kind of arrangement is imposed on hostile and unwilling parents? The evidence is not decisive. Weitzman suggests that the effect is likely to be further litigation, conflict, and extended and increased harm for children. But a study in California found that relitigation was less frequent after joint custody even where this was imposed by the court (Ilfield *et al.*, 1982).

Weitzman's reasons for opposing the trend to joint custody in California extend well beyond the question of children's relationships with their parents. She argues that joint *legal* custody (whereby the child is in the care of one parent, but both parents share the power to make decisions about the child) gives fathers yet another advantage in the legal battles that may surround divorce, since the father is given continuing power to interfere in his ex-wife's life with the children, and perhaps may also threaten to go for custody of the children himself as a weapon in a fight over property. (In the vast majority of cases, joint legal custody leaves the children living with their mother.) Other researchers are much more optimistic about joint custody than Weitzman, but agree that she has shown how women are disadvantaged at divorce by lack of money and power.

The debate over custody arrangements is likely to continue for some time yet, and much more empirical evidence is needed. It is clear that diminishing conflict between the parents, and a continuing relationship with both, contribute to a better outcome for the children. The character and circumstances of divorcing families differ so greatly that it would be surprising if one formula worked for all custody and access arrangements. A variety of solutions may be possible for different families. But are there boundaries to what is psychologically sound?

Psychological theory

While the amount of research on children and divorce has grown in the last five years, there is still a scarcity of good empirical data. Perhaps more important from a psychological perspective, there is as yet a lack of a general developmental theory that would set the various studies in a coherent framework. Developmental psychology has had far more to say about the development of mental abilities through childhood than about the emotional growth and needs of children in the context of home and family. The most influential of such theories as we have tends to be based in the psychoanalytic tradition – notably the work of Goldstein, Solnit and Freud, and John Bowlby.

Joint physical custody arrangements of the sort outlined above are contrary to the position taken by Goldstein, Freud and Solnit in *Beyond the Best Interests of the Child* (1973) and *Before the Best Interests of the Child* (1979), on the basis of psychoanalytic thinking. These two well-known and extremely influential books argue for the child's need for continuous care by autonomous parents. According to their theory, a child's relationship with a father is very much a function of the relationship the child perceives between the mother and the father. When this relationship is one of conflict, and when the relationship with the father is on an intermittent visiting basis, the father cannot be an effective 'psychological parent'. The child may even (according to this theory) be better off without any contact at all, to safeguard the crucial relationship with the 'psychological parent' – almost always the mother. These authors argue also for minimal intervention by the state in the arrangements parents choose to make for their children. However, as the psychologist Martin Richards (1986) has shown, such arrangements may be made in the interests of the *adults* involved, and their interests may conflict with those of the child.

An emphasis on the relationship between a mother and child, with secondary importance accorded to father–child and, more broadly, family relationships, runs through the bulk of developmental psychology up until quite recently. The work of John Bowlby in this vein has been particularly influential, emphasizing the importance of the bond between a mother and an infant. The literature on separation anxiety has led to overnight visits to the father by infants and toddlers being discouraged no matter how close their relationship.

Work in the psychoanalytic tradition has undoubtedly produced valuable insights into the consequences of divorce for children. One such insight is that the child's sense of time is quite different from an adult's. A few weeks can be a very long and significant time in the life of a young child, and decisions about placements need to reflect this. However the theoretical and empirical base for the recommendations made has been seriously questioned. It would certainly be a mistake for legal decisions and procedures to be based on them without attention to the limitations of the psychoanalytic approach. Richards has stressed, for example, that often psychoanalytic ideas are stated to be universal, yet the patients from which these ideas are derived form a very selected social group in a few industrial societies. Most analytic writing, he points out, assumes traditional western family and social arrangements, which may restrict its applicability to household arrangements that fall outside this tradition — such as one finds in say, the kibbutzim or the contemporary post-divorce household.

The boundaries of psychologically satisfactory child rearing situations are still being established through empirical research. The limitations of the psychoanalytic approach and internal disagreements amongst analysts, cast doubt on such generalizations as the child's need for the continuous presence of an omniscient parent, and the importance of a positive contact between two parents if a child is to maintain a beneficial relationship with both. In the last decade attachment theory has come under attack, partly for this emphasis on mother–child relationships, and more broadly conceived studies of family relationships have begun to look at the whole network of family relationships.

The effects of divorce compared with the death of a parent

Although a satisfactory theory is still lacking, clues to the important factors in reactions to divorce can be gained by comparing the effects of marital separation with the effects of other superficially similar situations such as the death of a parent; and by examining the situations that arise after divorce in more detail.

A finding that emerges again and again is that the death of a parent has far less severe and less long-term effects than marital separation; and the effects are of a different kind. This suggests that it is not simply the loss of a parent through divorce that is significant to a child, but the fact that this loss results from conflict between the parents and the apparent abandonment involved in the choice of one parent to live elsewhere. It is significant that the reaction of a child to a parent's suicide, which may seem like voluntary abandonment, far more closely resembles reactions to divorce.

Research by Michael Wadsworth and Mavis Maclean (1986) has shown that the long-term consequences of divorce as compared with the death of a parent, can reach far into adulthood, and are apparent in the level of education and income of men and women who as children experienced the divorce of their parents. They analysed data from a national cohort study of 5,362 children born in March 1946 in Great Britain, and followed at intervals of two years through childhood, then five years in adult life. The results showed that children of divorce were significantly less likely than other children (including children who lost a parent through death) to achieve educational qualifications. They were also more likely to have changed their social class in a downward direction during childhood and not to have recovered from this drop later in life.

These effects were slightly less where parents remarried, suggesting that the family's financial position is involved. So-called 'reconstituted families' tend to have a higher standard of living than single-parent households headed by a woman. The economic consequences of divorce cannot be separated from the psychological effects. A family in poverty cannot provide a happy and secure base for a child's intellectual and emotional development. Indeed, Wadsworth and Maclean use the notion of a 'happy family line' in income (which is considerably higher than the so-called 'poverty line') below which happiness is not likely to be possible for the family. Again and again studies show that for the great majority of divorcing couples, the financial consequences, especially for those who become and remain a single parent, are devastating. In the Maclean and Eekelaar sample (1983) over 80 per cent of couples had assets of less than £500 at the time of divorce.

Divorce for the children's sake

It has sometimes been said that divorce is better for a child than continuing a bad marriage. Unfortunately neither divorce nor an unhappy marriage is congenial to children, but there is little support for the notion of divorcing for the children's sake. Less than 20 per cent of the children in the Wallerstein and Kelly study experienced the divorce as bringing any kind of relief. Children have been found to fare better when their parents remain in a surprisingly cold or conflict-ridden marriage than after separation. Obviously there are extremes where a child will prefer and benefit from a separation. But even where there has been intense fighting during the marriage there is no guarantee that divorce will end it. As one child put it 'They said it was going to be better. But it's not, it's worse' (Kelly, 1984). Moreover, the possible benefits of divorce must be seen against the crises, disruption, psychological stress, and financial hardship it may bring.

It might be thought that through remarriage a new more harmonious and satisfactory family can be created. However, while again there are obviously cases where it works very well, remarriage is in general less beneficial to children than has often been supposed. Indeed, if it has any effect at all on the children's adjustment to their situation the evidence we have indicates that it is more likely to be a negative one. There is no support for the idea that the missing parent can in any real sense be replaced, nor that a stepparent can, by adopting the role of father or mother, readily become a child's new 'psychological parent'. Indeed, the attempts of a stepparent to adopt an absent parent's role is something children frequently mention as a reason for disliking him or her, and not getting along well. Yet this view that a parent can be replaced seems to account for the fact that it was, until recently, very rare for a man to get custody unless he could produce a new partner (or failing that, at least a female relative). Interestingly, Richards has suggested that the most successful stepparent–child relationships occur when the child retains a good relationship with the non-custodial parent. There is no evidence that for children to accept a stepparent a break must be made with the non-custodial parent. On the contrary, a good relationship with the father is more likely to permit a good relationship with a stepfather to develop.

Taking all these factors together it is clear that the notion that divorcing and possibly remarrying may be for the psychological benefit of the children is sometimes highly questionable. Set against this, it is important to remember that remarriage may alleviate financial difficulties. But children of divorce are, as Joan Kelly puts it, for the most part, unhappy and unwilling participants in what is essentially an adult solution to an adult problem. Divorcing parents must acknowledge this and recognize that their children's needs and wishes may well diverge greatly from their own.

Children and divorce: summary and conclusions

Deep distress at their parents' divorce is almost universal among children of all ages. In some cases the negative consequences are lifelong. Cultures, social groups, and family circumstances differ so greatly that there are serious problems about generalizing from the results of a few research projects. But certain central findings emerge consistently that have implications for the treatment of custody of children in law.

It is clear that general rules, such as mothers make the best mothers, or that divorce is better for children than an unhappy marriage are less sound and universal than was thought. Remarriage cannot easily replace an absent parent in a child's life, though it frequently has economic advantages which in turn create happier family circumstances. The importance to many children of their continued relationship with both parents comes out very strongly. Its importance has not been widely reflected in judicial attitudes to non-custodial parents, which has been described as one of indifference.

Children adjust better when the custodial parent is emotionally stable. The degree of continuing conflict between the parents affects a child's long-term adjustment, especially when the conflict involves the child. Counselling and divorce conciliation can reduce conflict in some cases, and the growth and development of these services should be encouraged. It is increasingly clear that the psychological effects of divorce are closely linked with its economic effects. As well as reducing continued stress, arrangements for children of divorce need to do whatever possible to protect them from the economic disadvantages.

While there are good reasons for encouraging divorcing couples to settle matters between themselves, their own interests and those of their children may conflict. It is virtually certain that separation will involve a period of anger and bitterness, during which access to a child may be opposed or made difficult by the parent with whom the child is living. The child's opportunities to maintain contact may need to be protected through an initial period if the child is not to lose contact altogether. From the child's point of view there is no merit in moving towards easier divorce. Martin Richards strongly urges that counselling should be available that could help parents to work out alternatives to divorce. Where divorce is inevitable counselling can help parents to understand their children's reactions and perspective and make the best possible arrangements for them by appreciating for example, that the continued commitment of both parents is (usually) going to be of great importance to a child; realizing the extent of the stress that is being placed on their children, and responding to their need to be talked to and kept informed.

One possible consequence of divorce may be an increased risk of delinquency. It is to this I turn next.

JUVENILE DELINQUENCY

The topic of juvenile delinquency is vast. Research in the area has been very comprehensively reviewed by Michael Rutter and Henry Giller in *Juvenile Delinquency: Trends and Perspectives* (1983). This section draws extensively on their book, but it is possible here only to have a brief look

Table 5.1. No. of offenders as a percentage of the population by age group (England and Wales).

Age	Males	Females
10–13	3.1%	0.8%
14–16	8.0%	1.7%
17–20	7.0%	1.0%
21 or over	1.3%	0.2%
All ages	2.3%	0.4%

(Source: Home Office)

at what has been learnt about the nature, causes and possible prevention of delinquency. The involvement of psychologists in the assessment of children coming before the juvenile courts is discussed in Chapter 7.

The scale of the problem

A rather high proportion of young people in the UK is coming before the courts. About one in five males has been convicted by the age of 20, and many more formally cautioned by the police. However, the offences are often quite minor, and about half of these youngsters do not appear before the court again. Even amongst recidivists, there is a dramatic drop in convictions amongst young men in their early twenties, when many stop offending. This pattern is reflected consistently in crime statistics. Table 5.1. shows the proportion of offenders in England and Wales in 1984 found guilty of, or cautioned for, indictable offences as a percentage of all their age-group.

Thus as many as 8 per cent of males aged 14–16 were convicted or cautioned, as compared with 1.3 per cent of males aged 21 or over. Over half the males found guilty of or cautioned for indictable offences were under 21. If we look only at offences of burglary and criminal damage, about two thirds of offenders were under 21. Known offending amongst females is much lower than amongst males, but follows a similar broad pattern of increase in adolescence and decrease thereafter.

Self-report studies, in which people are asked whether they have committed offences (whether or not they entered official records as a result), show that some degree of delinquency is so common as to be almost universal in adolescence. This raises the question of whether it makes sense to talk about 'delinquents' as a group at all. It does seem, however, that there are marked differences between non-delinquents, the 'transient' delinquent who ceases offending in early adult life and the recidivist who continues to offend. While in many youngsters delinquency is a passing phase, in some it is a persistent problem. These tend to be youngsters whose delinquency is more serious, and who started delinquent activities comparatively early. It is also more likely that for them delinquency is part of a broader pattern of social difficulties. In terms of individual, family and social factors associated with delinquency, transient delinquents are more similar to non-delinquents than to recidivists.

What then, are the factors associated with delinquency?

Individual factors

Sex differences. It may be that certain individuals are predisposed towards delinquency, because of their particular personality, or their sex. Although it is well known that females are far less prone to delinquency than males, the reasons for this are not fully understood. No doubt girls get away with delinquent acts more readily than boys, or in other ways are treated differently by the criminal justice system, and therefore feature less prominently in the statistics. But this is not a full explanation. Is the difference due to sex differences in aggression? Research has consistently found males to be more aggressive in their interactions with their peers from a very early age. Research also strongly suggests this has a partially biological basis, since the difference applies across many cultures and a wide age range and is found also in primates. It is also known that hormones (androgens and testosterone) have an effect on aggression — again suggesting a biological basis for the sex difference.

Another difference between boys and girls is the greater vulnerability of boys to family discord and stress. This has been shown in several studies, including studies of children of divorce referred to above, which show greater and longer-lasting effects of divorce on boys than on girls. Antisocial behaviour in boys, but not girls, is much more common where there is severe marital discord. It may be, of course, that girls show the psychological scars of serious family discord or breakdown in other ways, or at a later date. Other contributing factors may be the different behaviour of parents and others towards boys and girls, and the fact that it is usually the father who is absent when a marriage has broken down. Fathers may have special salience for boys.

Although the causes of delinquency do seem to be different in boys and in girls, unfortunately rather little is known at present about delinquency in girls. What follows therefore relates almost exclusively to boys.

Intelligence. Delinquency is consistently associated with lower intelligence. There are two likely explanations for this. One is that low intelligence means poor school attainment, which in turn leads to a sense of failure, low self esteem, and antagonism to school, which may contribute to delinquency. There is good evidence to support this argument at least in some cases, but it cannot explain why the link between low intelligence and antisocial behaviour exists in children from as young as three years old; nor can it explain cases where the antisocial behaviour pre-dates scholastic failure. The explanation here may be that both low intelligence and antisocial behaviour share a common cause, either within the individual or in the family circumstances. The question requires further investigation.

Other individual factors. A few studies have looked for associations between antisocial behaviour and a number of other physiological and psychological measures. One measure is skin conductivity, which is equivalent to measuring slight changes in the amount of sweat on the skin. Normally, a fright, emotional reaction, or other arousing stimulus results in a leap in conductivity of the skin. This is one of the measures used in lie detection tests (see Chapter 2). There are indications that lower skin conductivity and lesser reactions to a noise may be found in some anti-social boys. This parallels results with adult psychopaths, and also hyperactive children. There are suggestions also that antisocial children may respond less readily to 'punishment' in learning experiments, and may be more 'stimulus seeking', readily becoming bored, fidgety, and inattentive.

If further research does produce more conclusive findings they are most likely to be useful in explaining delinquency in those for whom it constitutes part of a broader antisocial personality disorder, which persists into adult life, rather than in those for whom it is a passing phase.

Family influences

Family influences come out very strongly in the research evidence. Rutter and Giller are unequivocal:

> the most important variables associated with both juvenile delinquency and adult criminality include parental criminality; poor parental supervision, and passive or neglecting attitudes; erratic or harsh discipline; marital conflict; and large family size.

The question is not, as these authors point out, *whether* these factors are related to delinquency, but rather *how* these influences operate. A fruitful approach has been close observation of families, to pin down particular aspects of family interaction. For example, parents of 'problem' children tend to issue more commands to their children, and to engage more in coercive interchanges with them. It has been found that parents of normal children can make them behave more badly by issuing more commands. Moreover, altering the coercive approach of parents of problem children has proved successful in reducing the children's social aggression.

The most striking link with delinquency in children is the parents' own criminality. It may have long since ceased, but the relationship is stronger if it continues into the time of the children's upbringing. It is unlikely, however, that children's delinquency is often a result of direct imitation of their parents. It is more likely that criminality in the parents is associated with a cluster of other factors, such as failure to supervise children, drinking problems, violence, unemployment, and other family factors that are in themselves important in giving rise to delinquency.

It is clear that family discord, expressed in a variety of ways, is important, but again it is not yet clear what aspects of this are crucial. For example, it could be the stress of living in a quarrelsome unpleasant family atmosphere or it could be weaknesses and disruptions in family relationships. These are difficult to disentangle, but both seem to play an important part. The research on divorce confirms that changes in family relationships, for the better or for the worse, are paralleled by changes in the children's behaviour.

Looking within the family is sometimes the most appropriate way of tackling delinquency in individual cases. Detailed studies within families can reveal the social learning processes whereby children acquire a repertoire of social behaviour, and treatment can then seek to change destructive patterns.

Films and television

I raise the question of the effects of films and television only briefly. Their influence, if any, is extremely difficult to tease out — not least because the effect could go either way, promoting or reducing aggressive or violent behaviour and attitudes. It may seem that violence on television or in video nasties must surely have an effect on young people exposed to it. But it is extremely difficult to design and carry out research that sorts out just what is cause and what is effect. It is also difficult to establish what people have actually watched. Youngsters claim to have seen films that do not exist, casting doubt on their claims to have seen others that do exist. Direct imitation does sometimes occur, but usually a combination of factors has led to it and it cannot be blamed simply on a film or programme. On the evidence so far films and television appear to be of relatively small importance in the context of other factors associated with delinquent behaviour.

Responses to juvenile delinquency

Is juvenile delinquency to be understood and responded to in different terms from adult criminality? The answer is both yes and no. The research clearly supports the notion that juveniles who come before the courts should be dealt with not only with a view to the seriousness of the offence, age, and previous record, but also taking into account social welfare concerns and needs. For the vast majority of minor cases these latter concerns should probably be left aside. For most, delinquency is a temporary phase during adolescence associated with negative or unhappy circumstances of one kind or another, which passes when the circumstances change or the adolescent grows up. However, given that most adult criminals begin their criminal careers as juveniles, there are clearly some common causes, at least for this group. These seem to be a mixture of more extreme levels of the same predisposing factors as apply more generally, with more long-term individual characteristics such as serious personality disorders in a 'hard-core' of offenders.

Unfortunately, the court has no way of knowing whether a particular individual is one of those who will not re-offend anyway. The question for the criminal justice system is, can anything can be done to sway the balance away from re-offending; and is there a danger of making matters worse by the wrong sort of intervention?

Rutter and Giller argue that a policy of minimal intervention is appropriate with first offenders and for minor offences. Most such offenders will cease offending without any intervention in any case and there is a strong chance of making matters worse. They recommend that informal community interventions should be encouraged as the first resort, to convey firm disapproval of the behaviour, and to encourage the responsibility of the offender and his family. If this kind of response is not successful, it can be stepped up by stages. The next steps are formal police cautioning, and those judicial responses which sanction and deter with a minimum of active intervention, such as fines or adjournment. It is important to resist the temptation to do too much. Research by Ian Berg (1979) and his colleagues on truancy has shown that a simple adjournment of the case, with reappearance contingent on school attendance, is a far more effective way of getting children back to school than a supervision order involving the social services. The steps continue through an attendance centre order for more serious cases, to more intensive intervention.

For a small subgroup of offenders, therapeutic interventions are appropriate. These are offenders who desire help for their emotional problems or those for whom delinquency is part of a broader pattern of social difficulties. Residential placements will sometimes be needed, to remove the offender from a damaging family environment, or to control very serious or dangerous activities. But there is very little evidence that such placements are beneficial in the long term.

This stepping-up of intervention might seem to be pretty close to what the police, magistrates and judges do anyway. However, this is not always the case. Police cautioning for example, could be used less readily, and the form that community programmes and residential placements take is not always the most appropriate. Cairine Petrie's study (1984) of 'List D' schools in Scotland paints a depressing picture of boys from deprived backgrounds who commit relatively trivial offences for which they are sent to institutions which she describes as 'expensive anterooms to the prisons'.

Juvenile delinquency: summary and conclusions

Research has established that certain individual and environmental factors can accurately predict a high risk of delinquency. Children who go in and out of children's homes or foster care, or who come from families where there is serious marital discord, low parental supervision, poor housing, poverty or violence – all form 'high risk' groups. Males are more likely to become delinquent than girls, as are less intelligent children. Less is known about the mechanisms underlying all these links.

The vast majority of those who commit criminal offences as teenagers spontaneously cease offending by their early twenties. Too much intervention by the criminal justice system can easily make matters worse. Therapeutic interventions are appropriate for a few. Intensive intervention is inevitable for some. For most, given our present state of knowledge, the best that can be done is to intervene as little as possible, and wait for them to grow up.

In conclusion . . .

Conclusions have already been drawn after each of the three main sections in this chapter – children as witnesses, children and divorce, and juvenile delinquency. Two further more general points can be added.

The first is that the courts are clearly, and not surprisingly, somewhat frightening places for many children. Ian Berg's studies of truancy show that this may be an advantage in dealing with some juvenile cases. But there is a strong case for less formal settings for cases where the child is a witness, victim, or subject of a custody dispute.

The second is that in many cases involving children it is simply not possible for a psychologist nor anyone else to evaluate alternatives objectively nor to predict the outcome of different courses of action. The courts are faced with impossible decisions. How these dilemmas should be solved are questions not for psychology but for society. Psychologists may, however, help clarify the dimensions of the problem.

References

Berg, I., Hullin, R. and McGuire, R. (1979) A randomly controlled trial of two court procedures in truancy. In D.P. Farrington, K.O. Hawkins, and S.M.A. Lloyd-Bostock (ed.) *Psychology, Law and Legal Processes*. London: Macmillan.

Davies, G.M. and Flin, R. (1988) The reliability of children as witnesses. In *The Child Witness: Do the Courts Abuse Children?* Leicester: Division of Criminological and Legal Psychology of The British Psychological Society.

Goldstein, J., Freud, A. and Solnit, A.J. (1973) *Beyond the Best Interests of the Child*. New York: Free Press.

Goldstein, J., Freud, A. and Solnit, A.J. (1979) *Before the Best Interests of the Child*. New York: Free Press.

Goodman, G., Jones, D.P.H., Pyle, E.A., Prado-Estrada, L., Port, L.K., England, P., Mason, R. and Rudy, L. (1988) The child witness in court. In *The Child Witness: Do the Courts Abuse Children?* Leicester: Division of Criminological and Legal Psychology of The British Psychological Society.

Hetherington, E.M. (1981) Children and divorce. In R.W. Henderson (ed.) *Parent–Child Interaction*. New York: Academic Press.

Ilfield, F.W., Ilfield, M.Z. and Alexander, J.R. (1982) 'Does joint custody work?' *American Journal of Psychiatry*, 139, 62–66.

Kelly, J.B. (1984) Children of divorce: At separation and five years later. In S.M.A. Lloyd-Bostock (ed.) *Children and The Law*. Oxford: Centre for Socio-Legal Studies.

Maclean, M. and Eekelaar, J. (1983) *Children and Divorce: Economic Factors*. Oxford: Centre for Socio-Legal Studies.

*Mitchell, A. (1985) *Children in the Middle*. London: Tavistock.

Petrie, C. (1984) A comparative study of boys in 'open' and 'closed' compulsory residential placement. In S.M.A. Lloyd-Bostock (ed.) *Children and The Law*. Oxford: Centre for Socio-Legal Studies.

*Richards, M.P.M. (1986) Behind the best interests of the child: An examination of the arguments of Goldstein, Freud and Solnit concerning custody and access at divorce. *The Journal of Social Welfare Law*, March, 77–95.

*Rutter, M. and Giller, H. (1983) *Juvenile Delinquency: Trends and Perspectives*. Harmondsworth: Penguin.

Spencer, J. (1987) Child witnesses: Video technology and the law of evidence. *Criminal Law Review*, February, 76–83.

Wadsworth, M.E.J. and MacLean, M. (1986) Parental divorce and children's life chances. *Children and Youth Services Review*, 8, 145–159.

*Wallerstein, J.S. and Kelly, J.B. (1980) *Surviving the Breakup: How Children and Parents Cope with Divorce*. London: Grant McIntyre Ltd.

*Weitzman, L.J. (1985) *The Divorce Revolution: The Unexpected Social and Economic Consequences for Women and Children in America*. New York: The Free Press.

Further reading

Publications marked with an asterisk (*) above.

Burgoyne, J., Ormrod, R. and Richards, M. (1978) *Divorce Matters*. Harmondsworth: Penguin. [Chapter 4 is recommended.]

Davies, G.M. and Drinkwater, J. (ed.) (1988) *The Child Witness: Do the Courts Abuse Children?* Leicester: Division of Criminological and Legal Psychology of The British Psychological Society. Occasional Paper No. 13.

Lloyd-Bostock, S.M.A. (ed.) (1984) *Children and the Law*. Oxford: Centre for Socio-Legal Studies.

Chapter 6

Communication Skills Out of Court

Most solicitors spend only a small proportion of their time in researching the law or attending court; but a very large proportion of their time is spent interviewing and dealing with clients, or negotiating with other parties. Little is done to prepare lawyers for this aspect of their work. As Avrom Sherr puts it:

> the tenor of those [four or five] years of legal training will have been to train the students how 'to think like a lawyer' but not how to act like one. The application of legal principles, comparing and distinguishing cases and looking up the relevant law will be almost second nature. It is therefore a little frightening to realise how small a part this sort of work plays in a normal practitioner's life. (Sherr, 1986a)

It does indeed seem that lawyers, including very experienced lawyers, often lack basic communication skills. To borrow a term from the computer world, lawyers are not 'user friendly'. Poor communication was one of the most important reasons for clients' dissatisfaction with lawyers revealed by the Benson Committee on the Provision of Legal Services, which reported in 1979. Research has also found widely differing outcomes of negotiations from one lawyer to the next in simulation exercises. This suggests that lawyers vary greatly in their negotiating skills, and that some perform rather badly.

This chapter will be the most 'how to...' one in the book, because there are tried and tested techniques of interviewing and handling social interactions that work for lawyers, as they do for doctors, managers, teachers, clinical psychologists, and the many other groups who have been trained successfully. Much is also now known about what makes written language easier to understand. From this work, guidelines have been derived that can transform the comprehensibility of legal language without sacrificing precision or subtleties of meaning.

The skills of interviewing, negotiating and drafting each need a book to themselves to be fully covered – and indeed several books exist, notably Avrom Sherr's *Client Interviewing for Lawyers: An analysis and guide* (1986b), and several 'how to negotiate' books such as Roger Fisher and William Ury's *Getting to Yes* (1981). In the US there is now an extensive literature on these skills. What I can do here is outline the basic psychological principles involved, and show how these translate into quite specific guidelines for conducting interviews, communicating clearly, and negotiating efffectively. While these techniques are usually easily understood, putting them into practice effectively is unfortunately a different question. Reading this chapter is not in itself going to make anyone into a skilled interviewer or negotiator. Mastering any skill requires practice. Ways of starting to put these ideas into practice are suggested at the end of the chapter.

INTERVIEWING

A complex skill such as interviewing brings together several different areas of psychology. Most prominent is the psychology of *social interaction and social skills*, which is developed, for example, in the work of Michael Argyle at Oxford (Argyle, 1975). A great deal is now known at a detailed level about the kinds of verbal and non-verbal behaviour that affect the way an encounter will develop. People talking and listening to each other are not only processing the substance of what they are hearing and saying, but also constantly monitoring each other's cues and signals, and changing their own behaviour in response to them. Thus, for example, they will respond to encouraging signs of interest by saying more. This may seem obvious, but it is surprising the extent to which one person can influence what, how, and how much another will say. There have even been studies claiming to show that the frequency with which particular words are used can be increased by giving small signs of encouragement such as a smile and a nod each time the word is used.

From close study of what these ways of talking, cues and signals are and their effects, it has been possible to develop specific questioning techniques for particular purposes: methods of putting others at ease; ways of increasing co-operation and compliance; and in general more effective ways of achieving the aims of an encounter.

The second relevant area of psychology is that of *information processing*. At the same time as monitoring these various signals and responding to them, people are obviously to some extent processing the substance of what is said – both by themselves and by the other person. Here another set of considerations come into play that are very relevant to lawyers' interviews with clients, especially a first interview. We do not take in everything we hear. Nor do we understand it in a vacuum, but rather we bring past experience and expectations to bear on it. Unstructured information is much harder to cope with, and people tend to impose an at least provisional structure on incoming information early on. Thus, a lawyer interviewing a client is likely to form a working hypothesis very quickly as to what sort of a case it probably is, and what sort of a client, and to understand what the client is saying in the light of the hypothesis. One of the commonest mistakes made by solicitors in client interviews is to pigeon-hole a case too readily, and as a result, fail to pick up important information. Avrom Sherr, in his research on lawyers' interviewing, found their most common error was rushing to a preliminary view of what is important, and concentrating all efforts on a very narrow view of what seems to the lawyer to be legally relevant.

Unfortunately experience is, if anything, likely to make matters worse. With experience people such as lawyers, doctors, and aircraft pilots acquire skill at diagnosing problems. Their skill develops by building up in their memory a repertoire of types of cases encountered and their outcomes. New cases then do not need to be puzzled over from scratch, but can rapidly and unreflectively be classified as examples of a class that the lawyer (or whoever) has available in memory. The person has 'seen the situation before', and 'knows' how to respond. Most of the time such a strategy is extremely efficient. Experienced doctors, for example, diagnose not only much more quickly, but also much more accurately, than less experienced doctors. It does, however, have precisely the drawback that Sherr and others have noted: a tendency to pigeon-hole too readily, perhaps idiosyncratically, to decide action along well-worn grooves, and to be blinkered to features of a case that do not fall into a typical pattern. This applies to negotiations between lawyers as well as to dealings with clients. Similar situations will come round again and again, and repeat players at negotiation will have acquired skill at responding to them. But rules of thumb will not always work. (See my discussion of how sentencers classify and respond to cases in Chapter 4.)

Advantages of skilful client interviewing

A lawyer who is easy and pleasant to talk to will have happier clients, but that is not the only advantage. If interactions with clients are handled well, there is evidence that the result will be more effective handling of cases, more co-operative and competent clients (who pay their bills), and less time wasting, for example through phone calls from anxious clients who remain dissatisfied or uncertain after an interview.

Barriers to communication will obviously hinder the process of finding out what has happened to bring the client to a lawyer, and of exploring fully the ways in which the lawyer may be able to help. Even if it is a 'simple' matter of conveyancing, good communication is essential. Not only can time and hassle be saved on the immediate matter of the conveyance. Avrom Sherr notes that people often move house at a crucial stage in their lives (such as marriage or divorce, retirement, moving job, or having children). Buying a house is often the first reason a client has for contacting a lawyer. It is quite possible that there is other legal work, such as drafting wills, that could arise out of these events. Or the satisfied client may come back for the conveyance on a later house move – on average after seven years.

Sources of difficulty

There are several likely sources of difficulty to be overcome in communication between a lawyer and a client. One, as we have already seen, is the tendency of lawyers to use legal pigeon-holes too readily. Another may be the client's unfamiliarity with legal concepts and language. (This is perhaps less of a problem for some kinds of commercial work, for example.) A third may be the client's anxiety. For some kinds of cases a certain amount of anxiety may be unavoidable, but excessive anxiety can interfere with people's ability to process information. Nervousness or irritation can detract from a client's ability to tell the story or to take in and understand advice. Upset or anxious medical patients for example often do not take in much of what a doctor is telling them.

If clients are to get across what they want to say it is therefore very important that they should be put at ease as far as possible, and given every opportunity to tell the story in full. When it comes to putting a legal framework to the case and giving advice, it is important that this is done in a way that can be assimilated by a client who may have come into the interview with a very different framework of interpretation.

Physical surroundings

Much can be done before an interview even begins in order to set a favourable atmosphere and reduce barriers to communication. The reception area of an office is an important part of a client's first impressions; Sherr comments that it would be a strange clientele that was *really* interested in two-year-old copies of *Punch* on the table, together with the latest editions of *The Law Society's Gazette*. Other suggestions include redecoration and a few potted plants to brighten up a dowdy area, facilities for children (if appropriate), coffee and tea, and clear signs to the toilets.

If attention is paid to these kinds of things, the interview itself can begin with a client who already feels welcome and physically comfortable, who has positive expectations, and whose anxiety has been kept to a minimum.

The room where the interview is to take place is similarly worth attention. Books on how to be successful make much of the ways in which power can be expressed in room layouts. A large imposing desk facing the door and standing between the occupant of the room and any visitor is one way of emphasizing the superior status and power of the occupant and of keeping visitors in their place. A lower, and uncomfortable chair for the visitor is another. Of course, these effects are counter-productive in client interviews. A layout which suggests an equal partnership is much more conducive to talk and co-operation. Managers often have a couple of similar and comfortable chairs and a low table in a part of the room away from the desk, where visitors can be seen. If this is impractical a useful idea often used by doctors is to arrange things so that the lawyer and the client sit at right angles to each other, with the client at the corner of the desk. The lawyer can then continue to use the desk, but the desk does not act as a barrier between them.

Opening the interview

Avrom Sherr found that an astonishingly high proportion of new articled clerks fail to greet clients properly. Many remain seated behind their desks rather than greeting the client at the door, and fail to make a proper introduction. If clients are to be at ease it is, of course, important to maintain ordinary politeness and consideration – taking their coats, introducing oneself and anyone else in the room, showing clients where to sit, and so on.

If a client is to get across what he or she wishes to say it is very important to set the right pattern from the start of an interview. For reasons already outlined, a first interview should begin with a chance for the client to tell his or her story with as little contribution to the talking from the lawyer as possible. Research has shown that the proportion of time each person spends talking during the first five minutes of an interview establishes the 'floor-taking' pattern for the rest of the interview. The client must therefore be allowed and encouraged to embark on telling the story without interruptions or hindrance from the lawyer. Obtaining specific pieces of information, such as the client's personal details, are much better left until later. It is difficult to switch from the question and brief answer pattern this sets. Market research interviewers are trained to leave personal details to the last because they are not relevant to the subject matter of the interview. The interview proper cannot get going, and this is frustrating for the respondent. Moreover, such information as age and occupation is somewhat private and more readily given after rapport has been established.

Eliciting the story in the client's own words is chiefly a matter of asking broad, *open-ended* questions, followed up by *active listening*.

Types of question

The most important verbal interviewing technique is the appropriate use of open-ended or closed questions. Open-ended questions are ones to which it is difficult to give brief replies, such as 'How can I help you?'; 'What has happened since then?' They usually begin with words like 'What . . .?', 'How. . .?', or 'Why. . .?' 'Why' questions have to be used with more caution than 'How' or 'What' questions. A question such as 'Why did you do. . .?' can easily evoke defensive feelings. Other open-ended questions that work well take the form 'Could you tell me about . . .?', or 'Can you describe an example of that?' This allows plenty of scope for replying in different ways.

Clearly there are degrees of open-endedness. Even after the client has said what he or she wants to say initially, slightly more focused (but still open-ended) questions can be asked.

Closed questions have the effect of limiting how much the other person will say. More closed questions are used to make someone speak less, to keep the talk to the topic in hand, and to extract specific information. This is normally appropriate to later stages of a first interview. Their stultifying effect is softened if they are prefaced by an explanation of why the information is being requested even if this is very general. 'It may be helpful to know whether there were other witnesses to this. Did anyone see. . .?'

Pauses

Most people dislike silence in conversation or discussion, and will feel a growing urge to fill a silence by speaking themselves. If the other person does not start to answer a question quite quickly, or pauses before the answer is complete, it is very important to have the confidence to wait. Especially when an open-ended question has been asked, clients may need a few moments to gather their wits. All the good work of an open-ended question will be undone if it is followed up, before the client has time to answer, by a more straightforward, but closed question.

An interview can sometimes in fact begin with a pause, instead of an open-ended question. If the lawyer simply looks encouragingly at the client, the client will probably start to talk. However, a hesitant client will need to be invited more explicitly to speak before the silence becomes uncomfortable.

Reflections and summaries

A second verbal technique, that shows you are listening and following, is *reflecting*. This is saying something that reflects back what the other person has just said, possibly using some of the same words. It may begin 'So. . .'. Overuse of reflections can produce an irritating, parrot-like effect. But used with discretion this can be a good way of handing back the talking to the other person with reassurance that you are listening, and encouragement to continue.

Reflections do not come naturally, and need practice. One pitfall is to parrot part of what the other person has said – probably the last part – but fail to reflect accurately the main idea, or the essence of what was said. An extract from an interview quoted by Sherr (1986b) illustrates how a reflection can indicate understanding without interrupting the flow of what is said. The following exchange occurs after the client has said she went to court to obtain access to her son.

1 *Client:* I got it and I went down, picked him up and this was the first time I'd seen him after 18 months and he still remembered me and was quite happy to come away with me. And when we actually got to the bus stop I thought if there is going to be any sort of hassle about him coming away with me it's going to be when he realises that he's actually going to get on the bus with me . . .
2 *Lawyer:* Mm.
3 *Client:* and come away with me and I was quite, I was quite um happy about, well not happy about, but I accepted that if he said "No" you know I won't have to push it.
4 *Lawyer:* You might have to take him back.

5   *Client:*   Yes, well in actual fact the woman that my husband lives with, Gwen, came to the bus stop and made quite a big show of "Bye bye Daniel" and Daniel said "Bye bye" and off he walked. . . .

The lawyer's comment at 4: 'You might have to take him back', accurately reflects the essence of what the client has been saying, and shows encouraging interest and understanding without affecting the flow of the client's story.

Reflection of content can also be used to summarize an interview or part of an interview and pull together the essence of a number of a client's statements. Summaries allow the speaker an opportunity to correct any misunderstanding the listener may have of what has been said. Lawyer–client interviews are special in that it is essential to make certain that the facts and the client's wishes are fully understood before any advice is given or action taken. There needs to be a specific stage of summarizing and checking. (Surprisingly, Avrom Sherr's research has shown that lawyers often do not check the facts fully with clients before proceeding to advise.) Sometimes note taking can be integrated into the interview at this stage. Notes the lawyer has made can be referred to, or even read out, and revised after any correction.

Because a full check will mean the lawyer taking the floor and doing most of the talking for a while the client may easily be discouraged from coming back with corrections or reinterpretations. If the summary casts the facts in terms of what the lawyer sees as legally relevant, this too may make it difficult for a client to correct misunderstandings. The lawyer will no longer be reflecting and summarizing, but interpreting and drawing inferences within a frame of reference that may be different from the client's. Skilful summarizing and checking is important for sustaining the client's feeling of having said what he or she wanted to say, and having been sympathetically understood.

Other techniques

A number of other verbal techniques indicate that you are listening and interested. A major one is the use of positive reinforcers, such as 'Yes', 'Good'. Another is reference to the other person's past statements, such as use of their name, or reference to their ideas.

Non-verbal techniques are often a wordless equivalent of verbal reinforcers. Signals that encourage the other person to talk include smiles, nods, eye contact, 'mhmms', and an attentive posture. In ordinary conversation we naturally look at someone to let them know we are interested in what they are saying. However, during an interview people tend to look at their notes or at documents. Note taking is vital. The fuller and better the notes, the less room there is for misunderstanding as the case develops. But the amount of time looking away from the other person is best minimized, and the effects of not looking so much at the other person must be compensated for by increasing other signals of interest.

Gaze is also an important regulator of turn taking in conversation. Looking away to take notes may upset this mechanism. While we are listening we normally look at the speaker. While we are talking we tend to look away from the person we are addressing, only glancing at them from time to time. If a speaker maintains continuous eye contact whilst speaking, the effect is somewhat aggressive. When the speaker wishes to hand the talking back to the listener, he or she looks at the listener as a signal that it is the listener's turn to speak. This sudden prolonged gaze is the *regulator*. Other regulators include a change in intonation, a drawl on the last syllable, ending of a gesture or relaxation of a tense fist, and a decrease in the loudness or pitch of the voice. Looking away from the speaker signals that you would like a turn to speak. If these various regulators are used poorly, a conversation will not mesh. There will be interruptions, overlaps, and other misunderstandings, and rapport will not build up. If a lawyer looks away to take notes or refer to papers, the client may stop talking, or feel uncertain whether the lawyer is still listening. A positive effort is needed to keep the interview flowing whilst taking notes. As well as using signals of continued interest, it helps if the lawyer mentions at the outset that he or she plans to make some notes.

Clues to others' feelings

Most people are familiar with the idea that 'body language' can give us an idea of a person's motives, feelings, or intentions. It may be helpful to be able to pick up clues that a client is feeling stressed. People often try to control the emotions they show in their faces, and most people can do so quite successfully. However, it seems that this control in some way bottles up emotional energy that finds its release elsewhere, in a fidgeting hand or foot. As an interview comes to a crucial point from a client's point of view, a kind of *non-verbal leakage* may occur (compare the discussion of clues to lying in Chapter 2). Posture is also, of course, a clue to how stressed someone is. A stiff upright sitting position and folded arms almost always indicate that someone is not relaxed.

Other barriers to rapport

Questioning style and other techniques affect how the other person feels about the interview as well as the quality of the information elicited. I have been suggesting that one barrier to communication is to take too active a role in directing what the other person says, for example, by using closed questions. As well as limiting the information that can be obtained, an interrogating style can make the other person feel as though he or she is 'in the dock' and always responding to the listener's probing.

Several other ways of interviewing can also arouse negative feelings, and are barriers to listening. One important group concerns lack of sympathy for the other person's feelings: not accepting the other person's feelings, making evaluative statements, appearing puzzled by their behaviour, or seeming to humour them. Acting in a patronizing manner or putting on a professional façade also makes for poor rapport. Lastly, there are ways in which the interviewer may impose too much interpretation on what is being said: labelling or diagnosing the other person's behaviour, suggesting explanations that bear little relationship to what they might have thought of by themselves, and not giving the other person the opportunity to make his or her own decisions. Of course, if a client has gone to a lawyer for advice, then he or she wants and expects advice and a legal interpretation of events. But giving advice can be reserved until the last part of the interview, and can be given in such a way that the client is presented with choices and the information to help make them.

Giving advice

I have stressed the importance of allowing and encouraging a client to tell the story in his or her own words, with a minimum of direction from the lawyer. When it comes to giving advice the lawyer obviously must take over most of the talking, and take control of the interpretation being put on the facts. Again, there are two aspects to consider: making sure that the client understands and can remember what is said; and making sure that the client continues to feel he or she is being sympathetically and respectfully treated and is involved in the process of deciding on any further steps to be taken.

Advice will be better understood and remembered if it is structured in an organized way, in much the same way as a lecturer might structure a lecture. A good technique for a lecturer is to set out in advance the broad headings that will be covered, and then refer back to this plan as the lecture progresses. A similar approach can be useful in interviews to give a frame of reference into which the client can fit what the lawyer is saying. Thus, the lawyer might say something like: 'First let me outline the general legal position in cases like this; then we can look more closely at how the law applies in your case; and after that decide what steps to take'. If the relevant law, or the consequences of taking certain steps are in themselves complex, these can in turn be further broken down in advance. For example, before discussing possible steps to take, the lawyer might say something like: 'There seem to be three main alternatives: x, y, and z. Let's look at what each would involve.'

If a client is to comply with advice or a plan of action, it is obviously necessary that he or she should agree, with some certainty, with the course of action chosen or advised. This agreement needs to be based on a full understanding of the steps to be gone through, the probable time scale and costs, and any areas of uncertainty and anxiety likely to be encountered. What and how much needs to be said at this stage of course depends on the kind of case. But even in a straightforward conveyancing case the client needs to know what to expect, and rapport can be strengthened if the lawyer shows concern for the client's possible feelings of anxiety or frustration. If it is not possible to decide on a course of action without further information, then that also needs to be made clear.

The interview as a whole

Avrom Sherr draws together the various stages and tasks of an interview helpfully in Table 6.1.

These stages and tasks are in a common-sense sequence, but in practice they are often jumbled, skimped, or missed altogether. Table 6.1. highlights that listening is an important phase to be distinguished from questioning. It emphasizes the importance of checking, repeating and recounting, of ensuring clarity about the next steps to be taken, and of ordinary politeness. The list of tasks can be used as a checklist for assessing your own interviews after they are over.

NEGOTIATING

Most solicitors have to play the role of negotiator. In civil cases, in particular, there is usually a possibility of arriving at a negotiated settlement.

Table 6.1. First interview: the thirteen tasks by stages.

Listening	1. Greet, seat and introduce. 2. Elicit story with opening question etc. 3. Listen carefully to basic outline of personalities and case from client's own unhindered words.	6. Note taking
Questioning	4. Question on facts for gaps, depth, background, ambiguities and relevance. 5. Sum up and recount lawyer's view of facts, *and* check for client's agreement or amend.	
Advising	7. State advice and/or plan of action and deal with question of funds. 8. Repeat advice/plan of action *and* check for client's agreement or amend. 9. Recount follow-up work to be done by client. 10. Recount follow-up work to be done by lawyer. 11. State next contact between lawyer and client. 12. Ask if "Any Other Business" and deal with it. 13. Terminate, help out and goodbye.	

Reprinted with permission from A. Sherr, *Client Interviewing for Lawyers: An analysis and guide*. Sweet & Maxwell.

Tough or co-operative?

Research and writing on how to negotiate contains a running debate between those who argue for a *co-operative* approach and those who argue for a *tough* approach. There is considerable evidence that most negotiations in practice fall into one of these two categories. Competitive, or tough, negotiators are characterized by a forceful, attacking approach, making a high opening demand, being willing to use threats or 'stretch' the facts, and not revealing information. Co-operative negotiators, in contrast, adopt a friendly manner, take a more realistic opening position and are willing to move from their original position. They avoid using threats, and are willing to share information. Whereas competitive negotiators tend to see negotiation as a game and delight in getting the better of the other side, co-operative negotiators are interested in a fair settlement for their client.

At first glance it would seem that these two types are 'hard' and 'soft'; and that a soft bargainer up against a hard bargainer would always lose. However, this is not the case. There are effective and ineffective negotiators of each type, and each approach has its advantages and disadvantages.

Gerald Williams's empirical studies in the US of how practising lawyers actually negotiate provide interesting information on this. Hundreds of lawyers in Denver and Phoenix were asked to complete a questionnaire about their recent negotiating experiences, and personal interviews were carried out with 45 lawyers. Over 100 cases were monitored as they progressed, and a small sample of lawyers were videotaped negotiating hypothetical cases. Unfortunately this is at present the only large scale empirical study of its kind, and many of the results relate only to one group of lawyers in Phoenix. It is therefore rather uncertain how generally applicable they may be. In addition, questionnaires to lawyers about other lawyers' negotiating performance is a method with its limitations. None the less, some central findings are of interest here.

The two negotiating patterns outlined above were clearly identified. The majority of lawyers (65 per cent) were co-operative, while 24 per cent were competitive in approach. (The remainder did not fall into any clear third pattern.) Neither approach, however, had a monopoly on effectiveness, though a higher proportion of the effective negotiators were co-operative (as rated by other lawyers) rather than competitive. Williams suggests that it may be more difficult to be an effective competitive negotiator than an effective co-operative one.

His analysis distinguishes the characteristics of effective and ineffective negotiators within the two categories. Thus, ineffective competitives are described as irritating, headstrong, unreasonable, arrogant, devious, and obstructive. Williams (1983) writes: 'The problem of the ineffective/competitive is easy to define: he is obnoxious!' The effective/competitive, however, is seen as experienced, realistic and perceptive. Effective negotiators of both types have some features in common. Both are seen as experienced and ethical. Both observe the niceties of custom. Both are realistic, fully prepared, astute, perceptive, and skilled at reading their opponent's cues. Ineffective co-operatives have many socially desirable traits, but lack perception, and are not convincing, realistic or rational.

What makes negotiating strategies work?

How, then, do each of these two approaches work? The main ingredients of a tough approach as analysed in the social psychological literature include making high initial demands and maintaining a high level as negotiation proceeds, and making few, and small, concessions. These tactics are often effective, resulting in a better outcome. However, their effectiveness depends on the information and experience of the negotiating opponent. If an opponent has no clear idea of what a claim is worth, the initial demands of the other side will serve to anchor these perceptions and contribute to setting the opponent's own goals. If, however, the opponent is well informed and experienced, and already has clear goals then the opening demands of the other side can be used to assess their reasonableness and to recognize the strategy being adopted.

Being prepared. The effectiveness of a competitive or tough strategy is thus limited by the preparedness of the other side. Hazel Genn has shown this in personal injury litigation. In that context, it is very often the plaintiff's solicitor who is at a disadvantage against the defendants. The plaintiff's solicitor is likely to be less well informed about the facts of the case because the opportunities and resources available will be less than those available to insurance companies. Insurance companies can often begin to assemble information from an early stage as if the case might eventually go to trial. A plaintiff's solicitor will come on the scene much later, and with fewer resources for, say, an engineer's report. Thus knowledge of the strength of the case is often very uneven between the two sides. In addition, insurance companies have extensive experience of similar cases, and have a better basis for working out what a claim might be worth if it goes to court, and what the plaintiff is likely to settle for. The consequence, according to Genn, is a serious disadvantage to the injured person in personal injury cases.

An extreme illustration of this kind of disadvantage is found if one looks at settlements made directly between the defendant – say an insurance company – and the injured person. Research at the Centre for Socio-Legal Studies in Oxford (Harris *et al.*, 1984) found that when this happens damages are often severely discounted. For example, one man who went straight to the driver's insurance company after a road accident accepted a first offer of £600, yet he was seriously and permanently injured, and spent 30 weeks off work. The research found that accident victims had virtually no idea what their claims might be worth and normally relied on lawyers to tell them. Nor did they realize that it is customary to negotiate over such claims, but assumed that there was a going rate for these things, and that the insurance company (or local council bus company, or whoever) could be relied upon to pay the appropriate amount.

Solicitors, one hopes, are not so naïve. But it is clear from Hazel Genn's research that the clients of solicitors who do not specialize in personal injury work are far less likely to do well out of their claims. The research at the Centre for Socio-Legal Studies also suggests that non-specialized solicitors do not always know the ropes of personal injury negotiation, and may be more ready to recommend acceptance of an early offer.

Time. One kind of information that can be crucial in negotiations is knowledge of each other's time constraints. This may be a relevant factor in some legal negotiations. A ploy said to have been used by Japanese business men against overseas visitors who come to discuss a business deal is to find out at once when their return flight leaves. The visitors are then lavishly entertained, taken on tours, and so on, while the time available for negotiations ticks past. By the time the hosts finally consent to get down to business discussions, their visitors are frantic to reach some kind of agreement before they have to leave.

Emotional significance. These various aspects of knowledge, experience and preparedness relate to comparatively objective aspects of negotiation – the ability of each side to weigh up accurately the worth of a case to each side and the costs and benefits to each side of settling. The other aspect of negotiation is its emotional significance. Negotiation itself involves costs and pay-offs for the people involved, in such terms as stress, power, loss of face, sense of victory, and so on. The major drawback of the competitive approach is that it increases tension and mistrust between negotiators. This can distort communication and lead the two sides to believe they are further apart than they in fact are. It can build up resentment and an inclination to bloody-mindedness in an opponent. Negotiations are more likely to reach an impasse. In Williams's study, competitive negotiators failed to settle and went to trial substantially more often than co-operatives. Interestingly, *ineffective* competitives in this study tended to *settle* more often than ineffective co-operatives. Williams suggests that ineffective competitives are bluffing their way through but are not legally astute or prepared. They therefore tend to 'chicken out' when going to trial becomes a real possibility.

Settlement vs. trial. As Williams points out, there may be nothing wrong with a high trial rate from an attorney's point of view. It may be that a tough negotiator gets better settlements, but the price is a higher trial rate. However, since trials are costly, those clients whose cases go to trial may do less well out of a tough strategy than those that settle. A tough strategy may mean sacrificing the best settlement in some cases for a better settlement on average.

The possibility of going to trial may, of course, loom differently for each side in the negotiations. Settlement in personal injury cases provides an example. As Hazel Genn's study has shown, insurance companies are likely to be better prepared to take a case to trial if it should come to that. Their threat to do so is therefore more likely to be real. Moreover, an insurance company is usually in a position to 'win some and lose some', while for the plaintiff, the particular case is what matters. The plaintiff will therefore be inclined to settle rather than risk going to court. The risk that tough tactics may lead to a breakdown in negotiations is thus both lower and less threatening to the defendant than to the plaintiff. A tough approach is what one would predict from insurance companies in these circumstances – and indeed that is what Genn finds.

The 'problem solving' approach to negotiation advocated by Fisher and Ury in *Getting to Yes* (1982) is largely aimed at avoiding the drawbacks of tough negotiation. A central tenet is 'separate the people from the problem'. This means separating the substance of the negotiation from the relationship with the other side; allowing the other lawyer to save face; concentrating on good communication and not responding to threats and attacks. They suggest a negotiator should be 'hard on the problem; soft on the people'. The negotiating strategies expounded in *Getting to Yes* have been used as the basis of negotiation training for a wide range of negotiation settings. One useful aspect of their approach is their emphasis on analysis of the problem and creativity in looking for solutions that may maximize the interests of both parties. The weakness of the co-operative approach which Fisher and Ury seek to avoid is its vulnerability to exploitation by the other side. If a co-operative negotiator continues to make concessions, and share information in the face of a competitive negotiator who does not reciprocate, the co-operative negotiator is at a disadvantage. Fisher and Ury emphasize that negotiators, while refusing to enter into or respond to personal attacks, must not give in to threats, but insist on reason and objective criteria.

Whatever broad strategy may be adopted, many of the same kinds of interpersonal techniques discussed above in connection with interviewing are relevant also to negotiating. The same factors that inhibit or facilitate communication in interviews apply also in face-to-face negotiation. For example, as in client interviews, stress and emotional involvement can hinder ability to understand and communicate. The use of silence may be particularly effective in getting the other side to speak, and thus make a move.

Negotiators are often advised to avoid making the first offer, as this means showing their hand to some degree. This applies more where the other side already has clear goals: otherwise there may be advantages in getting in first and setting the area of negotiation in a favourable region. Proposals advanced later in a negotiating session are much more likely to be accepted than proposals advanced early on.

Rather than debating whether a competitive or a co-operative strategy is in general more effective, it is more useful to draw out the factors and approaches that make for effective negotiation, whatever the general approach. We have seen that the most important factor is preparedness. This includes having relevant information about the particular case, as well as the more general knowledge and experience to assess what a realistic settlement might be, and what form the customary process of negotiation tends to take. On this basis, goals and strategy can be worked out. As Hazel Genn's study shows, a solicitor who lacks sound information and is not experienced in the type of case is unlikely to get far against an opponent who is well prepared and experienced.

Experience of negotiating is more likely to lead to effectiveness than is experience at interviewing. This happens largely because there are clearer criteria of success, and more feedback about how successful a negotiation has been. As seen in Chapter 4, experience without feedback can simply lead to idiosyncracy and an inflated view of one's own skill. A solicitor in a small firm that does very little personal injury work, and who never realizes that a settlement was far from the best that could have been achieved, is not going to improve much as a result of the experience. One who realizes he or she has been bluffed, bounced, or caught unprepared, is more likely to be able to do better next time.

The client's eye view of negotiation

One of the complaints sometimes made about lawyers by clients is that they immediately see everything in terms of the law and legal solutions. To go to a lawyer is therefore to get caught up in a legal merry-go-round that has a momentum and logic of its own. Of course, in a sense lawyers are there to do precisely this. Clients would surely complain if lawyers did not interpret and pursue their clients' wishes and needs in legal terms. But it is important for lawyers to remember that using the law is often in itself a significant, often confusing, and possibly hostile or vindictive thing to do. As well as this, lawyers, like it or not, have considerable power to influence how their clients view the rights and wrongs of a situation, and to affect their beliefs about what they are morally entitled to. A client may depend on a lawyer not only to give legal advice but also to structure the client's perceptions of what has happened and what can be accepted as putting things right.

These points are well illustrated by my own research into accident victims' perceptions of fault and liability for their accidents (Lloyd-Bostock, 1979). It was clear that the way in which victims attributed fault, and what compensation they felt they were due, was powerfully influenced by their involvement in a compensation claim — even the *possibility* of a claim had an effect.

In domestic and leisure accidents, where claims for damages are very rare, the overwhelming majority of accident victims blamed no one else for their accident and never considered the question of compensation. But in road and work accidents, where there is a high possibility that someone will suggest making a damages claim, almost half the victims blamed someone else. What is more, they blamed the person or organization they would most likely be claiming against — the driver in road accidents or their employer in work accidents. In work accidents this usually meant attributing fault in terms of poor management, working conditions, and other background factors rather than more immediate causes such as someone else not paying attention.

A clear conclusion was that tort law structures when and how ordinary people attribute fault for their accidents and what they perceive as a just outcome. Factory inspectors confirm the malleability of victims' perceptions of their accidents. Victims are often said to be poor sources of information for inspectors on how the accident happened. Interviewed too soon after the accident they have not yet worked out in their own minds what happened. But by the time they have, their views are influenced by what trade union representatives, lawyers, and others may have suggested about compensation. It is not that injured victims distort reality or deliberately try to cast events in a particular light. Many accidents can be explained and understood in a range of different ways. The blame for, say, a fork-lift truck accident might be placed on the driver, the supervisor, the employer, the manufacturer of the fork-lift truck, possibly others, or no one else at all. How much money a victim believes he or she ought to get in compensation is even more open to suggestion. The Oxford survey (Harris *et al.*, 1984) found that the amount a victim thought he or she should get was, with very few exceptions, a sum suggested by someone else — usually a lawyer.

The research also illustrated that taking legal action is in itself a somewhat hostile thing to do. Some victims who became involved in claims were very unhappy about it because of what they felt they were doing to the other party. Many, in fact, dropped their claims, or never brought one after thinking about it, because they felt that the other person had suffered enough already, had been very kind to them, or in some other way 'paid' already. Some saw it as not in keeping with their self-image to do something that vindictive.

As part of this research, 182 accident victims who obtained damages awards were asked for their views about the solicitors who had conducted the claims. Replies confirmed the general picture that in personal injury cases often the clients feel confused, buffeted and bitter. The most frequent complaint was that solicitors showed lack of interest in their claim. Others complained of the delay involved in claiming. Eight claimants reported having 'disagreements' with lawyers, and in every case the issue was the amount of damages. Claimants felt they were advised to settle too low. This is especially interesting when taken together with the fact that the clients' notion of the worth of the claim relied heavily on the lawyers' advice in the first place. These disagreements illustrate how the lawyers' advice as to how much they might get becomes internalized and viewed as what they *ought* to get. Subsequent offers will then be evaluated against this.

Another area where lawyers' negotiations have been studied is in divorce settlements. It has sometimes been suggested that lawyers create further division in matrimonial disputes, propelling couples into divorce and hindering amicable agreement. The empirical evidence we have, however, suggests that this is a misleading picture. Richard Ingleby of the Centre for Socio-Legal Studies in Oxford has recently made a study (as yet unpublished) of matrimonial cases handled by Manchester solicitors. There was no indication that going to a solicitor in any way hindered co-operative settlements or reconciliations. Solicitors spent a considerable amount of time dealing sympathetically with emotionally distressed clients, a high proportion of whom were suffering violence from their spouses. Undoubtedly there are some lawyers who take the 'hired gun' approach to divorce, especially where significant assets are at stake. But this image is largely irrelevant to matrimonial work in the vast bulk of cases both in the UK and in the US.

In summary, one of the things a lawyer needs to remember is that using the law in a dispute is in itself a significant thing to do – perhaps a hostile or vindictive act. This adds to the stress and anxieties surrounding legal action. Only a fraction of potential legal disputes get to this stage, and in those that do, the client may not wish for confrontation. Lawyers have considerable power to affect their clients' perceptions of events and their notions of justice. This places responsibility on lawyers to exercise this influence carefully.

USING CLEAR LANGUAGE

Legal documents are notoriously obscure and difficult to understand. Complex ideas do not necessarily have to be expressed in complex language. Often the application of a few basic principles and a little imagination can transform complex legal language into readily-understood English. Lawyers are accustomed to dealing with documents, and are familiar with legal jargon. Unless they make a deliberate effort to think about the needs of their non-lawyer readers, they are prone to produce what to the ordinary reader is incomprehensible legalese. It is worth remembering that an estimated two million people in the UK have a reading ability less than that needed to read the *Sun* newspaper.

Simple language is easier to understand than complicated language, but there is more to it than that. Comprehension is closely linked to perception and memory. Anything that affects one of these processes will also affect the others. Material that is quickly perceived is usually dealt with more efficiently in other cognitive processes. Anything that slows down these processes by adding extra cognitive work (such as unfamiliar words) makes language more difficult to understand.

One expert in communications has concluded that legal writers suffer from an occupational disease – a disease that is fortunately curable. Research into the psychology of using and understanding language has highlighted some forms of expression to avoid and others to favour. The research provides general guidelines only, and not hard and fast rules. Indeed, one reason people sometimes write poorly is that they are slavishly applying rules instilled by an English teacher, such as 'Never use the same word twice in a sentence'. The most important rule is to bear the potential reader in mind.

Commonly used words versus unusual words

Familiar words are more easily recognized, remembered, understood and used. Legal language characteristically includes many unusual words, or unusual uses of words. For example, the National Consumer Council (NCC) (1984) quote the following clause from a credit sale agreement:

> The property in the goods delivered pursuant to this agreement shall pass to the buyer on delivery.

The word 'pursuant' is unusual, while the words 'pass' and 'property' are used in unusual ways. This could have been written:

> You will own the goods as soon as they are delivered to you.

Concrete versus abstract words

Concrete information is grasped more readily and has more impact on people than abstract ideas and statistics. We see this clearly where the risk of danger is concerned. For example, a campaign is being conducted in Finland to reduce heart disease. As part of this campaign, schools are being persuaded to alter school lunch to a healthier regime. In one school there was resistance on all sides to any such change, despite the statistical evidence that the existing diet carried health risks. Then a teacher at the school dropped dead of a heart attack at the age of 42. The abstract risk was suddenly understood, and opposition to the changes vanished.

If legal writing needs to contain abstract ideas, concrete examples will increase comprehension. For example, one legal text explains the abstract concept of *volenti non fit injuria* (assumption of risk) as follows:

> If a person suffers harm after having consented expressly or impliedly to either of the following, he cannot afterwards sue in tort in respect of that harm.
> (a) If he agrees to somebody doing an *intentional act* that would otherwise be a tort.
> (b) If he agrees to *run the risk* of *accidental harm* that would otherwise entitle him to sue for the tort of negligence.
>
> If a man entered hospital to have his appendix removed, this would be an example of (a), for he would be agreeing impliedly to an act that would otherwise amount to the tort of battery. If he went to watch a dangerous sport such as motor racing, this would be an example of (b). The difference between (a) and (b) is that in the former the person gives his consent to harm that he knows *will* occur, while in the latter he gives his consent to harm that *may or may not* occur; he goes to hospital in order to be cut with a scalpel but he does not go to a motor race in order to be hit by a crashing car. (Sim and Scott, 1978).

The crucial ideas are italicized by the authors ('intentional act', 'run the risk', 'accidental harm', the difference between 'will occur' and 'may or may not occur') and are all made clear by concrete examples.

Expressing complex abstract ideas needs extra care in general, not just concrete illustrations. When people have difficulty understanding legalese, lawyers tend to assume it is primarily because the legal concepts are inherently difficult. There is some truth in this, but research has shown that complex abstract legal concepts can be made dramatically more comprehensible. As part of their study of jury instructions (see pp. 54–57) Robert and Vera Charrow asked attorneys to rate the complexity of the legal concepts involved in standard jury instructions. They found that the instructions attorneys rated as involving the most complex concepts were also the ones that improved most in comprehensibility when the researchers modified the language. It seems the attorneys' ratings were influenced by the complexity of the language as well as the complexity of the concepts. The explanation of *volenti non fit injuria* that I cited above, is a good all-round illustration of how clear language can make an abstract idea much easier to grasp. Where the explanation includes unusual words or phrases (such as 'consented expressedly or impliedly', 'the tort of battery') they are appropriate because the intended audience of law students needs to become familiar with legal terminology.

Homonyms

Homonyms are words that are spelt and pronounced the same, but have different meanings. For example, the word 'material' can be an adjective meaning 'physical', or an adjective meaning 'relevant' or 'important'; a noun meaning 'subject matter', or a noun meaning 'cloth'. Such words can cause confusion. If a lawyer uses the word 'material' to mean 'relevant', the chances are this will conjure up a fleeting image of 'cloth', since this is the most usual meaning. Even words that are only spelt alike (homographs) or pronounced alike (homophones) can be confusing. 'Converse', for example, may mean 'talk' or 'opposite' depending on how it is pronounced. Even if the meaning is easy to work out, such words tend to slow down or interrupt the flow of reading and understanding.

If homonyms cannot be avoided, the difficulty they may cause can be reduced by providing a strong clue as to which sense is intended before the word appears. Thus: 'As well as gymnastics, many pupils enjoy karate or fencing'. The meaning of 'fencing' is clear in this sentence. Compare it with the sentence: 'He spent the afternoon fencing'. Here no clue is provided. Or, 'He enjoyed fencing, but he preferred laying turf'. Here there is a clue, but it comes after the ambiguous word.

Synonyms

People sometimes use synonyms to avoid repeating a word in the belief that this improves their style. Sometimes it does, but sometimes it introduces unnecessary confusion. For example instead of 'There are three books in the series. . . . The first book deals with . . .' someone might write: 'There are three books in the series. . . . The first volume deals with . . .'. No one is likely to be seriously puzzled by this second version, but it is not an improvement. 'Book' and 'volume' have different shades of meaning. The use of 'volume' introduces unnecessary ambiguity as to whether the writer intends to make a distinction or not.

Sometimes legal writing goes in for strings of synonyms and redundant words or phrases, such as 'last will and testament'. This introduces confusion as to whether important additional information is being conveyed, or the same information simply being repeated for emphasis. The ordinary reader is unlikely to know whether or not a slight difference of meaning is important. The NCC (1984) produced a long list of commonly-used legal phrases which contain words of almost the same meaning. The list includes 'alter or change', 'cease and desist', 'full and complete', 'undertake and agree', 'made and entered into', 'null and void' (or even 'totally null and void and of no further force or effect whatsoever').

Negations and opposites

A negative sentence is more difficult to understand than an affirmative one. This is because it requires a two-stage operation. First the positive meaning has to be grasped, and then its opposite worked out. Thus the sentence: 'He was not honest', requires first an understanding of 'he was honest', and then of the negative of this sentence. Words such as 'never', 'scarcely', 'few', and 'minority' all increase comprehension time. Instructions are also best given in an affirmative form – 'Turn left only' rather than 'No right turn'.

Negations can take the form of *negative modifiers* – for example '*im*polite', '*un*caring', '*dis*honest'. These almost always make favourable adjectives unfavourable. There seems to be a general bias in talking and writing towards making favourable judgements, and there are more favourable than unfavourable adjectives in the English language. The opposite – using modifiers to make unfavourable words into favourable ones almost never occurs. Thus we use 'impolite' but not 'unrude'.

Research has found that negative modifiers make language harder to use and to understand. It is easier to understand an antonym of a different root – 'rude' rather than 'impolite', 'deceitful' rather than 'dishonest', 'contradictory' rather than 'inconsistent'. These negations again require a two-stage process of comprehension – understanding the positive concept, and then a negation of it. They are, however, generally easier to understand than negations of whole sentences. Thus, 'This is contradictory' is easier than 'This is inconsistent', but both these are easier than 'This is not consistent '.

Long and complex sentences

Short and simply constructed sentences are usually easier to understand. But length and complexity interact. A long sentence that is simply constructed can be easier to understand than a series of several shorter sentences. For example, 'After a few days in hospital she was ready to go home' may be easier to understand than 'She went to hospital. She was there a few days. Then she was ready to go home.' Compound sentences, made up by joining clauses with words like 'and' or 'but', are also comparatively easy to understand. They may help to avoid a jerky rhythm. It is sentences with embedded clauses that cause most difficulty. These are especially difficult if an embedded clause separates the subject of the sentence from the main verb, or the verb from the object. The NCC gives this example:

> This agreement, unless termination has occurred at an earlier date, shall expire on November 1, 1983.

Here the subject (this agreement) and the verb (shall expire) are separated by the distracting qualification 'unless termination has occurred at an earlier date'. The sentence is much easier to understand if those intervening words are moved to the beginning or end of the sentence:

> Unless it is terminated earlier, this agreement will expire on November 1, 1983.

Or again:

> The proposed statute gives to any person who suffers loss by reason of discrimination based on race, religion or sex a cause of action for damages.

Here, 16 words separate the verb (gives) from the object (a cause of action). This can be rewritten:

> The proposed statute gives a cause of action to any person who suffers loss by reason of discrimination based on race, religion or sex.

The difficulty rapidly increases if more than one subordinate clause is embedded in a sentence. As in the above examples, the problem is greatest when such embedded clauses split the main clause. For instance if we add another clause to the example above, it becomes even harder to understand:

> The proposed statute gives to any person who suffers loss by reason of discrimination based on race or religion, or who suffers loss by reason of discrimination based on sex, a cause of action for damages.

Active versus passive voice

Several researchers have argued that sentences using the passive voice lead to more confusion than those using the active voice. However, this confusion only arises if the subject and object of the sentence are logically interchangeable. Thus, 'The green truck is being pushed by the red truck' is confusing, but 'The leaves are being raked by the boy' is not. Used with care, the passive voice can usefully emphasize that the focal point of the sentence is the logical object. For example: 'The policeman was severely beaten by the intruders' is a sentence about the policeman, while who beat him is less important. The sentence, 'The intruders severely beat the policeman' has a different emphasis.

Using the passive voice often makes a sentence more wordy and less forceful. It needs to be used with care, but sometimes it will be more appropriate than the active voice.

Variety in style

A series of sentences of similar length and structure can have a very dull effect. But variety is not always an improvement. We saw above that repeating the same word can be better than deliberately trying to avoid repetition by using synonyms. The same applies to grammatical style. A repeated construction can be clearer than a varied construction, and can indicate that there are parallels in the content. For example, one researcher compared the following sentences:

> 1 'One group favours gradual desegregation while another demands that the integration be brought about immediately, and a third group said that it is altogether opposed to integration.'
>
> 2 'One group favours gradual integration, another demands immediate integration, and a third opposes integration altogether.'

The variety of structure and vocabulary in the first sentence is a distraction. The structure of the second sentence signals that each parallel section is about a similar topic, and highlights the actual differences between the three groups.

Organization and layout of information

Organization makes a great difference to how well people understand written material. As we saw in the context of interviewing, people can follow and understand much better if they are able to fit new information into a pre-existing structure. This can be achieved in several ways. A logical underlying sequence is important, and this will be picked up more easily if it is made explicit. Side headings can help greatly, provided they accurately and helpfully describe a document's content and structure.

As an alternative to a long sentence, it can be a good idea to tabulate information. Each item in a tabulated list should be marked, for instance with an asterisk. All items must belong together, and the penultimate should usually end with a semicolon followed by 'and' or 'or'. For example:

This fee will be refunded if:

* the employee withdraws before the starting date and no suitable alternative is found;

* the job is cancelled because of the employer's illness or death; or

* the employee leaves within three months.

Tabulating information is often a good way of making clear the conditions or exceptions attached to an agreement, or what will happen under a range of different circumstances.

FROM THEORY TO PRACTICE

Understanding the sort of techniques I have described is one thing but putting them into practice quite another. While they can most definitely be taught, it is a mistake to expect everything to come together quickly. Unfortunately, it is also true that experience does not necessarily lead to improvement (though I have stressed the benefits of experience at negotiation). So what steps can a lawyer take to improve interviewing, negotiating and writing skills? The need for legal skills training as a component of lawyers' training is being increasingly recognized, and some excellent programmes now exist – though these are still much too thin on the ground. In the meantime, there are some positive steps that lawyers can take on their own to try to improve their interviewing, as well as other skills.

There are two main reasons why communication skills are more easily understood than acquired. First, until a new technique becomes familiar, it will have to be deliberately practised. It is very difficult to interact with someone else and at the same time consciously monitor, evaluate and modify what is happening. It is especially difficult if several new skills are being attempted at once. No one with any sense would expect to learn to drive by reading a book about driving a car, and then getting in, and immediately attempting to drive along a busy road. The task needs to be broken down into manageable chunks and, if possible, each chunk practised with time to reflect.

Trying to acquire all the component skills of interviewing (questioning, listening, etc.) in one go is therefore too much to cope with. Even with videotape facilities, analysis of all aspects at the same time presents an overwhelming amount of information. It is much more feasible to concentrate on trying out particular techniques, such as asking open-ended questions, or reflecting. The techniques of questioning and listening can be tried out in conversation as well as in interviews. Programmed texts that take the reader through single skills in a step-by-step fashion can be successful alternatives to video analysis. No programmed text on interviewing has yet been prepared specifically for British lawyers, but several of the techniques I have described are taught through practical exercises in other contexts in *Essential Interviewing* (Evans *et al.*, 1979). A number of texts on legal interviewing have been written for US lawyers, sometimes including practical exercises. Examples are Schaffer and Redmount (1980) and Binder and Price (1977).

The second major difficulty is that of knowing how you are doing. As I have stressed before, feedback is essential for the development of a skill. Where steering a car, say, is concerned, the immediate feedback of the car's change in direction can quickly lead to the development of skill in steering. But how are lawyers to know how well they are interviewing, or writing? How are they to identify what components of their behaviour are producing which results?

It is a great help to watch oneself on video and have the comments and views of other people, specially people experienced in providing legal skills training. Videos not only allow us to see ourselves as others see us, but also let us analyse at leisure what went on in an encounter. 'Teach-yourself' methods without video are at a considerable disadvantage. But failing other opportunities, it is certainly possible to assess, monitor and improve one's performance.

Avrom Sherr concludes his excellent book *Client Interviewing for Lawyers* with some practical suggestions for planning, monitoring and reviewing the experience of new lawyers. He also provides practical checklists for monitoring interviews. The list of the 'tasks of the interview' given earlier can be used in this way. It is best if an interview is videotaped and a colleague can carry out the assessment. But the lawyer doing the interview can benefit from working through checklists after an interview, and recalling and evaluating his or her own performance. Particular tasks or techniques can then be practised and improved.

Writing stands a better chance than interviewing of improvements through experience and 'teach-yourself'. It is possible to just go ahead and try to apply guidelines on clear writing, because writing is a comparatively slow process allowing time to reflect and to check for comprehensibility. The publication *Plain English for Lawyers* (National Consumer Council, 1984) is set out in the form of useful guidelines.

Negotiating also stands a somewhat better chance than interviewing of improvement with experience, because 'knowing the ropes' is often so vital to success in legal negotiations. But we have plenty of evidence that drafting and negotiating skills are often very poor even among experienced lawyers. The skills of face-to-face communication needed for effective interviewing and negotiating are even less likely to be just picked up on the job.

Interviewing, negotiating and using clear language can all be dramatically improved for quite a modest investment of time and effort. Ideally these skills should be taught early in a lawyer's training or career (there is some debate about the exact stage at which such training is most useful). But much can be done at later stages and, if necessary, much can be self-taught.

References

Argyle, M. (1975) *Bodily Communication*. London: Methuen.

Benson Report. (1979) *Royal Commission on Legal Services Final Report*. London: HMSO.

Binder, D.A. and Price, S.C. (1977) *Legal Interviewing and Counseling: A Client-centered Approach*. St Paul, Minneapolis: West Publishing Co.

Evans, D.R., Hearn, M.T., Uhlemann, M.R. and Ivey, A.E. (1979) *Essential Interviewing: A Programmed Approach to Effective Communication*. Monterey, California: Brooks/Cole.

Fisher, R. and Ury, W. (1982) *Getting to Yes*. London: Hutchinson.

*Genn, H. (1988) *Hard Bargaining*. Oxford: Oxford University Press.

Harris, D., Maclean, M., Genn, H., Lloyd-Bostock, S., Fenn, P., Corfield, P., and Brittan, Y. (1984) *Compensation and Support for Illness and Injury*. Oxford: Oxford University Press.

Lloyd-Bostock, S.M.A. (1979) Common sense morality and accident compensation. In D.P. Farrington, K.O. Hawkins and S.M.A. Lloyd-Bostock (ed.) *Psychology, Law and Legal Processes*. London: Macmillan.

*National Consumer Council (1984) *Plain English for Lawyers*. London: National Consumer Council.

Schaffer, T.L. and Redmount, R.S. (1980) *Legal Interviewing and Counseling*. New York: Bender.

Sherr, A. (1986a) Clients are people too. *The Law Society's Gazette*, 26, November, 3563–3566.

*Sherr, A. (1986b) *Client Interviewing for Lawyers: An Analysis and Guide*. London: Sweet & Maxwell.

Sim, R.S. and Scott, D.M.M. (1978) *A-level English Law*, 5th edn. London: Butterworths.

Williams, G.R. (1983) *Legal Negotiation and Settlement*. St Paul, Minneapolis: West Publishing Co.

Further reading

Publications marked with an asterisk (*) above.

Chapter 7

Psychologists as Experts

Psychologists are becoming involved more and more often in legal cases. No one has actually kept figures, but it is generally agreed that the last 15 years or so have seen a dramatic increase in psychologists acting as experts, especially in the United States but also in the UK. The psychology professions have begun to recognize the need for special training for such work and some courses for clinical and educational psychologists now include a component on forensic psychology. Psychologists are also increasingly debating the ethics of this role (or roles). Some of the ethical dilemmas for psychologists are discussed later in this chapter.

It is important to stress that a psychologist acting as an expert should be qualified in the appropriate field. This may seem obvious, but there are many types of psychologist just as there are many types of lawyer. As we saw in Chapter 6, the client in a personal injury case will usually be well advised to go to a solicitor of some reputation specializing in this area. Similarly, a lawyer looking for expert advice or evidence from a psychologist will be well advised to look for the right kind.

TYPES OF PSYCHOLOGIST

The majority of psychologists who undertake legal work in the UK are clinical psychologists or educational psychologists. In a recent survey carried out by The British Psychological Society, over 92 per cent of psychologists who had given evidence in person in a court or tribunal were either clinical or educational. Both these professional groups have undergone postgraduate training in their fields and hold recognized diplomas or degrees.

Clinical psychologists work across a wide variety of areas of mental abnormality, including work with the mentally ill, the mentally handicapped, the addicted, those suffering from brain damage, the elderly, and disturbed children. They specialize within clinical psychology, but they will have received basic training in all the main areas. Forensic psychology is beginning to be recognized as an area of specialization within clinical psychology, but as yet the numbers are small. Most clinical psychologists are employed within the National Health Service. Some clinical psychologists working in regional psychiatry units now spend most of their time preparing evidence for court or appearing as expert witnesses. As forensic psychology develops as a specialized field within clinical psychology, this group of clinicians is likely to grow.

As their name suggests, clinical psychologists work with individual clients in a clinical setting; and their expertise is based not only on their scientific knowledge but also on their clinical expertise. Two matters of debate arise from this, that I return to later. Firstly they are professionals with responsibilities towards their clients. Involvement in legal cases can therefore raise dilemmas of professional ethics for them. Secondly, their evidence and advice is likely to be a mixture of the comparatively objective and the more subjective.

Educational psychologists similarly work with individual clients, and similar ethical dilemmas arise. But their field is much more closely defined. They are usually employed by a local education authority to work with children with educational difficulties. (Their counterparts in the US are known as 'school psychologists'.) As part of their training they will have qualified as teachers, as well as psychologists, and will have had teaching experience.

Their expertise is particularly appropriate when a child's developmental progress, adjustment, or ability needs to be assessed in juvenile court cases. This work probably represents the most extensive involvement of psychologists in legal cases. In a survey published in 1979, 45 per cent of educational psychologists stated that they had contacts with child or adolescent offenders at least once a month and 20 per cent stated that they worked in observation and assessment centres of social services departments at least once a month to provide psychological assessments of children who will go before the juvenile court. Since there are about 900–1000 educational psychologists in England and Wales, their work on juvenile cases represents a considerable amount of psychological input to legal decisions. Most of their input is either through their own written reports or their contribution to the report of another professional. Court appearances to present the report in person are comparatively infrequent.

Prison psychologists are a further group. They are sometimes trained as clinical psychologists, and, as their name suggests, they work with offenders in prison. They therefore often contribute to assessments of offenders, but they infrequently present evidence in court in person.

Occupational psychologists have expertise in such matters as recruitment and selection of personnel, management training and staff development and appraisal. Their contribution to legal cases is rare and is usually in the area of employment discrimination, or personal injury cases. There is no required qualification in occupational psychology comparable with those in educational and clinical psychology, but many occupational psychologists have undertaken postgraduate training or research in the field. An occupational psychologist will normally be qualified to administer and interpret psychological tests used in recruitment, careers advice and related areas. They often work on developing new tests for specific purposes.

Unlike educational, clinical and prison psychologists, occupational psychologists are employed in industry, or work in firms and partnerships of occupational psychologists, or are self-employed free-lance consultants.

Other groups of applied psychologists are less easily defined. Some work in research institutions such as the MRC Applied Psychology Unit at Cambridge University, or the Road Research Laboratory in Berkshire, or the Centre for Socio-Legal Studies at Oxford University. Often applied work is carried out by a psychologist in an academic post. For example, a cognitive psychologist interested in perception, information processing and decision making, might work in engineering psychology or ergonomics. He or she might therefore be able to provide expert advice on, for example, the adequacy of a safety system at work, taking psychological factors into account. Psychologists in academic posts working on memory and recognition have, in the US, given expert evidence on the reliability of eyewitness testimony.

Academic psychologists are primarily concerned with research and teaching in the universities and polytechnics. Clinical, educational, occupational, and other types of professional and applied psychologists are all found in university departments. So, however, are a great variety of other psychologists, most of whom do no applied or 'real world' research, nor any clinical work, but who engage in experimental research on questions of theoretical rather than practical interest.

Academic research in psychology covers many different specialist areas, from body language to the physiology of perception. Virtually every area has some actual or potential relevance and application to law. In previous chapters we have seen how research in perception and memory applies to questions about the reliability of witnesses; research in decision making to sentencing; physiological psychology to lie detection; child psychology to cases involving children; and social psychology to courtroom processes, legal skills, and the questioning of witnesses and suspects. However, it is important to remember that the vast bulk of research in psychology is carried out with no immediate practical applications in mind. In any area of psychology there will be research that is, as yet, of no practical relevance whatsoever. This is especially true of laboratory research that investigates theoretical questions. Most individual studies in psychology make a small contribution to a slowly accumulating body of research evidence, exploring a refinement of a theory or testing a possible explanation of apparently contradictory findings. Rarely, if ever, does one study alone provide information from which practical generalizations can be drawn. It is risky, therefore, to look at just a handful of studies to see what psychology has to say on a specific question. A knowledge of the research literature of which the studies form a part is needed.

While a particular question may arise in a legal case on which a psychologist engaged in pure research is qualified to offer an expert view, this type of involvement is rare. For example, a psychologist carrying out pure research into some aspect of brain function may be well qualified to give an opinion on the effects of a particular brain injury, but this kind of expert evidence is far more likely to be provided by a clinical psychologist specializing in neuropsychology. Academic psychologists are especially likely to be useful in cases where matters of principle are being discussed that go beyond the immediate case, and where the general corpus of knowledge therefore becomes more relevant. Such opportunities arise when an enquiry has been set up, such as the enquiry following the Confait case (see p. 25) where questions concerning the suggestibility of suspects with a mental handicap were central.

Psychologist or psychiatrist?

Many people get confused about the difference between psychologists and psychiatrists, and indeed, there are several areas of overlap in their work. They now frequently work together in multidisciplinary teams. However, psychiatry is a branch of medicine, and psychiatrists work within a career structure quite distinct from that of psychologists. They often treat the same disorders, and indeed the same patients, as do clinical psychologists. But as medical doctors, their approach tends to be more in terms of the diagnosis and treatment of mental disorders as medical conditions. They are qualified to prescribe drugs, and this often makes a considerable difference to the approach to treatment they adopt. Psychologists sometimes work with rather different theories and models, and therefore view behavioural problems in different terms. They may develop programmes of treatment involving no drugs, aimed at modifying behaviour. It may happen, for example, that a psychiatrist's evidence is more appropriate to *mens rea* issues and mitigation in a particular case, while a psychologist is the more appropriate person to suggest a treatment plan as an alternative to custody, or to provide evidence about intellectual abilities. In fields of psychology other than clinical psychology there is much less collaboration and overlap between the two professions.

ON WHAT ISSUES CAN PSYCHOLOGISTS ACT AS EXPERTS?

The kinds of questions on which psychologists give expert evidence are of course limited by what the courts will accept. At one time psychologists regularly gave evidence in obscenity cases, for example. In theory psychologists could still act in prosecutions under the Obscene Publications Act (1959) and in Scotland they still do from time to time. But in practice such work has virtually ceased in England and Wales following court decisions in the 1970s. The range of issues on which psychologists may act as experts is more restricted in the UK than in the United States. A notable example already mentioned is eyewitness testimony. In the UK the reliability of eyewitness testimony is regarded as a matter for the jury and ordinary common sense, and not for experts. In the US, however, psychologists have given expert evidence on this issue in many cases. The frequency with which they are doing so has increased greatly following Arizona and California Supreme Court decisions in 1983 and 1984 to overturn murder convictions in part because the trial court had excluded expert testimony on eyewitness identification.

None the less, there is a great range of questions on which psychologists in the UK have provided expert evidence; and in addition psychologists have acted in other more advisory roles in connection with legal

Table 7.1. Examples of the questions put to a clinical psychologist in legal cases.

1. Is the confession made by the accused likely to be genuine?
2. Did the plaintiff suffer brain damage; if so, to what extent? What degree of mental recovery can be expected over what duration of time?
3. Is the appellant a fit person to have the custody of his child returned to him? What is the present risk of physical assault against his children?
4. What psychological evidence is there to support the claim of the accused that the dazed condition noted by the police at the time of the accident was due to post-concussional confusion and not excess alcohol?
5. Can the recall of the 17 witnesses who have agreed to undergo forensic hypnosis, be improved by this technique to provide a more consistent and detailed description of a motor vehicle which the police wish to trace?
6. Is the person complaining to the police about obscene phone calls and damage to personal property manufacturing the evidence to satisfy psychological needs?
7. Is the suicidal risk present in this patient compulsorily detained in hospital on a Mental Health Order sufficient to justify her continued detention on the grounds of her own health and safety?
8. Is the mental condition of this patient sufficient for him to be detained under the Mental Health Act on the grounds that it is necessary for the protection of others?
9. What evidence can be offered to demonstrate the invalidity or unreliability of an uncorroborated statement by a police officer?
10. What evidence can be offered to demonstrate possible errors in the corroborated statements of two police officers?
11. What steps should the constabulary take to eliminate a weakness in a certain type of evidence?
12. What evidence is there that the physical condition complained of arises from the working conditions of the complainant?
13. What evidence is there to substantiate the statement of the accused that he was unaware of his conduct by reason of drunkenness?
14. What evidence is there that the accident arose from a genuine machinery hazard and not from carelessness?
15. Is there a sufficient *prima facie* case to plead against the carrying out of the death sentence on the grounds of insanity?
16. What evidence is there that customers confuse two different brands of a certain commodity and to what extent does this occur?

17. Are there any psychological factors relevant to the prisoner which would justify bail?
18. What psychological evidence of cruelty can be put forward to justify a plea for divorce on these grounds?
19. What evidence can be offered that the appellant is capable of managing his own financial affairs?
20. Can evidence of the effectiveness of the proposed treatment be sufficient to justify release of the prisoner from his prison sentence in favour of treatment under a probation order?
21. Can the plaintiff's probable future earnings be psychologically assessed?
22. What is the probability of the accused being schizophrenic? What evidence is there that he is insane?
23. What is the probability of the suspect having been a member of a proscribed political party and of arrestable rank?
24. What psychological evidence is available to show how suggestible children and mentally handicapped adults are, when interrogated by police officers?
25. What psychological evidence is available to show the validity of various methods of personal identification?
26. What defects exist in the medical evidence being put forward by the expert witnesses called by the 'other side'?
27. What are the psychological implications for the future of the party concerned in this particular case?
28. To what extent is the plaintiff mentally handicapped? To what extent is this handicap likely to affect his cycling skill? What is his probable loss of earning power, if any, as a result of the accident? What weaknesses, if any, exist in the medical evidence tendered by the witnesses for the defendant?
29. What was the perceptual basis of the Master's misjudgement in docking his ship?
30. Was the testator mentally capable of making a valid will at the time she did so?
31. What evidence can be offered as to the state of mind of the deceased shortly before death?
32. What psychological help can be offered to bring about a rapprochement and out of court settlement between these two litigants?
33. Are there psychological grounds arising from evidence heard at the previous trial and appeal which should be communicated to the House of Lords?

From L.R.C. Haward (1981) *Forensic Psychology*. Batsford. Reprinted by permission.

cases. Some idea of this range of topics and roles can be gained from Lionel Hawards's book *Forensic Psychology* (1981). Haward, a professor of clinical psychology, has experience of forensic psychology going back over 30 years, and has in many respects been something of a pioneer in this field. To illustrate the kind of problems that are posed for forensic psychology, he produced a selection of questions put to himself in various cases, and answered by him in the form of a written report, or proof of testimony, or in the witness box.

As the questions show, when clinical psychologists are engaged by lawyers it is usually in connection with the mental state or capabilities of their client. In criminal cases the questions are likely to concern the sanity, competency or dangerousness of an accused person. Some clinical psychologists also perform polygraph tests or forensic hypnosis and give evidence on the reliability of statements made by suspects (see Chapter 2).

A large slice of the clinical psychologist's forensic work is in civil cases, and especially in compensation cases where the victim has suffered a head injury. Neuropsychologists are frequently engaged in such cases to test the capacities of the injured person; to say whether any handicap or apparent reduction in capabilities is likely to have resulted from the injury in question; and to provide a prognosis as to the likely extent of future problems.

Educational psychologists, like clinical psychologists, are usually brought in to provide an assessment of mental capabilities, most often of children appearing before the juvenile court. Psychologists usually come into the system as agents of their local social services departments. They see the child, probably in an observation and assessment centre, and make a report. Occasionally a psychologist who has not seen the child (perhaps because access has been denied) is engaged by the 'other side' in a contested child care case to give advice at a general level about typical patterns of development and behaviour, or the interpretation of test scores. Andrew Sutton and Geoff Moss, two educational psychologists, have described and discussed in detail the role of the educational psychologists in the juvenile courts in this country (Sutton and Moss, 1984).

The cases educational psychologists become involved in include both civil and criminal cases. A care order may be sought in order to protect a child, or because the child has committed an offence. Or the issue may be custody of a child following divorce. The kinds of questions the psychologist will be concerned with involve both child and family, and their approach to assessment is similar whether the child is 'deprived' or 'depraved'. Is the child developing satisfactorily? What is the source of any problems and what might be likely to help? How would the child fare at a particular type of school?

Clinical as well as educational psychologists work on cases involving children, especially when the issues are clinical rather than scholastic or intellectual, and embrace the parents as well as the child. Clinical psychologists also work on High Court custody cases. Educational psychologists, as employees of the local authority, cannot usually appear for the parents. The emphasis in an educational psychologist's assessment is usually on intellectual ability, achievement and educational prospects. Standardized tests are almost invariably used, although as Sutton and Moss have pointed out, the recommendations made by the psychologist may bear no obvious relationship to the test results reported. The psychologist is drawing on information and experience that is not necessarily made explicit in a report.

Occupational psychologists have occasionally become involved as experts in discrimination cases. For example, an occupational psychologist might analyse the requirements of a job and express an opinion as to the qualities and skills required in an employee. The psychologist might, for example, say whether a requirement that employees pass an English language test is actually a reasonable requirement for that particular job, to help the court decide whether it amounts to racial discrimination.

Some occupational psychologists work 'behind the scenes' in tort cases, providing information to clinicians on employability and estimated future earnings following an injury. This information is then embodied in the clinical psychologist's report to the court.

Other kinds of psychologists have given expert opinions on a variety of matters. Specific issues include the comprehensibility of information provided with birth control pills; the likelihood that an average person would notice the warning on a can of lighter fluid; and whether two trade marks are likely to be confused by customers.

THE METHODS USED BY PSYCHOLOGISTS AS EXPERTS

Clinical assessment and psychological testing

The psychologist's contribution to a legal case is most often based on a clinical assessment of the individual concerned. The assessment is likely to include psychological tests of some kind. Psychological testing is a skilled task, and permission to use many of the published tests is restricted to specifically-qualified psychologists. Some tests (such as tests of interests and intelligence) are comparatively straightforward to administer and interpret, and most psychologists can, if they so wish, obtain and use them. The continued validity of these tests none the less depends on protecting their confidentiality. Other tests require much greater expertise and training. A battery of neuropsychological tests, for example, needs to be selected, administered and interpreted by a qualified expert in the field. Some tests of personality are quite straightforward to administer, but special skills are needed to interpret the test scores.

Three terms that are frequently used in describing tests and test scores are *norms*, *validity*, and *reliability*.

Norms are the yardstick against which test results are interpreted. Psychological tests of individuals embody the idea of comparing the individual's performance with that of other people – such as others of the same age. Norms allow this comparison to be made. They are developed during a process known as test standardization. At the early stages of constructing a test, no proper interpretation can be attached to the scores. The various items in the test may be good indicators of whatever the test aims to measure, but they need to be anchored and calibrated in some way. A thermometer that gives readings of 1–50 may be an excellent measure of temperature. But we need to know what the 1 and the 50 represent, and whether the numbers in between represent an even subdivision, or whether, say, the difference between 11 and 12 is larger than the difference between 20 and 21. Similarly, raw scores on unstandardized psychological tests are not possible to interpret.

The process of standardization does two things. It makes the scores statistically more convenient and it gives scores a meaning in relation to a standard, or normative group. As a result, an individual's score can be interpreted as, say, 'higher than the scores of 90 per cent of the relevant section of the population'. In order that this comparison can be made with the *relevant* section of the population, tests must be standardized on appropriate groups. Tests are frequently standardized on a range of age groups to permit age allowances, for example. A test standardized on a North American population may need to be standardized separately for use in the UK.

When appropriate, published tests are accompanied by a manual that contains conversion tables which enable a given individual's scores to be transformed to appropriate standard scores, by reference to norms. The same test may have different norms for use with different groups.

Validity is usually defined as the test's capacity to measure what it is supposed to measure. There are many different ways in which this can be tested or demonstrated. One method is to use criterion groups (such as one group of mental patients and another of people with no symptoms of mental illness) which the test should be able to distinguish, and see if it does. Because psychological tests measure intangibles such as 'intelligence', test validity is closely tied to psychological theory about, say, intelligence.

A related question is that of whether an appropriate test has been used. A test may be valid for certain purposes but inappropriate for others. For example, tests are designed with varying degrees of focus. A test may aim to produce a general measure of intellectual abilities, or a more focused measure of certain specific abilities. A test may be designed for use across a wide range of ability, or be designed to discriminate more finely amongst people within a much narrower range – perhaps the very able.

Something that people often find difficult to understand about psychological tests is how a particular item in the test can tell us anything about, say, a person's personality. The relevance of one item in isolation is not always obvious. There are several different approaches to the design and selection of test items and methods of analysing how they contribute to a test's validity. Items that do not improve the reliability or validity of a test are ironed out by these procedures. Interestingly, one of the *least* useful forms of validity is what is known as 'face validity' – that is, the test appears at face value to be measuring what it aims to measure. Face validity is, in fact, more likely to be a disadvantage than an advantage in personality tests, or any other test where subtlety and resistance to faking are important.

Reliability is the extent to which a test produces similar scores for the same person tested on several occasions. A certain amount of fluctuation from one occasion to the next is to be expected. But if a test purports to measure something stable and lasting about a person then results should not fluctuate too widely from one test session to another. Unreliability in a test can arise from several sources. One is trying to measure too much with too few test items. Another is ambiguity in the test instructions. Unreliability must be minimized in test design because it limits the possible validity of the test. However, any measure of human performance will vary to some extent from one occasion to another.

Sometimes, of course, psychologists want to develop a test that will measure things that fluctuate, such as mood, or change more gradually over time, such as a child's mental capacities. Reliability can still be established, for example, by comparing scores on one half of a test with scores on the other half at the same test session, or by testing on two occasions when no change is predicted on theoretical grounds. Often it is not desirable to use the same test twice to measure change over time, and parallel forms of the same test can be used.

The theory and process of test construction and validation are highly technical and complex and involve sophisticated statistical techniques. Many years work goes into the development of any widely-used test and a large literature is devoted to the subject of psychometrics. As well as psychological tests, psychologists may use physiological measures of some kind during their assessments. For example, they may use measures of sexual arousal to detect abnormal sexual responses. The interpretation of any tests or other measures will usually draw both on technical knowledge of the instruments used and on clinical experience of similar cases.

Special studies

Some of the most interesting contributions of psychologists to legal cases involve the psychologist in conducting special studies to investigate a specific question. Lionel Haward describes this as the 'experimental role' of the psychologist as expert. One study he undertook himself concerned a man who was seeking compensation for an injury at work. He had been working at a machine that was guarded in such a way as to prevent his right hand from becoming caught in the machine, but it was possible for his left hand to enter the danger zone. His employers argued that the machine was adequately guarded, since it was operated by the right hand: it was up to the worker to keep his left hand away as instructed. The worker argued that this was all very well while the job was being carried out slowly. But under pressure to keep up with the production flow his left hand automatically joined in, to clear obstructions in the machine.

Lionel Haward was called in as an expert to evaluate this notion of the left hand being used 'automatically' as the job was carried out more quickly. He did this by setting up a special study. A guard was designed that would exclude the left hand from actually being used to clear the machine. Subjects in the study were then set to work operating the machine under several different degrees of production pressure. Some operators could take it fairly slowly; others had to operate the machine at medium and faster speeds. Haward discovered that as the attempted speed of operation increased, so did a tendency for the left hand to rise towards the operating area to clear the machine for the following stroke. (This was futile of course, since the left hand was barred by the guard from playing any part.) Haward was able to conclude that when the injured worker was operating the machine, his left hand could well have been used automatically, and without conscious intent or awareness. As a result, the worker received compensation, and the guard designed for the study was turned into a design for a guard fitted to all similar machines to prevent a recurrence of this kind of accident.

Another study carried out to answer a specific legal question is described by Elizabeth Loftus (1986) in a case of trademark litigation in the US. The central issue was the possibility of confusion in the public mind between two bank logos. One bank was attempting to block registration of the other bank's new logo. Loftus was retained by the attorneys for the bank with the new logo to conduct a test of the potential confusion. She assembled samples of numerous bank logos used in the state of Florida, including the two banks involved in the dispute. Ten logos were assembled on one page and used in the study. Subjects were asked to say which two of the logos seemed to them to be most similar. When a black and white version was used only 1 out of 20 subjects selected the two logos in the dispute. When colour versions were used, 2 out of 20 selected the crucial two logos. On this basis Loftus concluded that the two logos were no more similar than other pairs of bank logos from Florida banks.

An additional study was conducted which did not involve side-by-side comparisons, since customers do not usually scrutinize logos in this way. In the first phase of this study, 10 subjects saw one of the logos, and 10 saw the other logo. They were told to look at it carefully as they would be tested later. They had three seconds to study it. The next day they were shown the whole page of logos and asked to pick out the one they had seen. Nineteen out of twenty of them picked the correct logo. The one subject who made a mistake confused the logo of the bank making the complaint with the logo of a quite different bank. A third study increased the interval to two days. This time two subjects made errors – but again, these did not involve confusing the two logos in question. (The outcome of the case, incidentally, was that the new management at the bank seeking to register the offending logo decided they did not like the new logo anyway and agreed to phase it out.)

The design and execution of special studies might be done by a variety of psychologists. Although Haward is a clinical psychologist, his clinical expertise was not essential for the study investigating the workman's claim that he used his hand automatically, mentioned above, which might equally have been conducted by a cognitive psychologist working in a university department or a research unit.

More general advice

Psychologists are sometimes called on to give expert advice based on their knowledge of psychological research, rather than their knowledge of a particular case. We have seen, for example, that a psychologist in the US might draw on research in memory, recall and recognition to give an opinion of the likelihood of an eyewitness making an error in identification. The advice may not be based on any specially conducted studies, nor clinical interviews with the particular witness, but rather on what emerges from the existing psychological literature on relevant issues. The value of such an opinion is limited in cases where clinical assessment would be more appropriate. But, in the right circumstances the right psychologist can give valuable advice at this more general level.

The advice of psychologists is also quite often sought by (or offered to) lawyers over matters of legal policy rather than individual cases. Psychologists have contributed to many Royal Commissions and Committees of Investigation, and their contribution is often published as part of the ensuing official reports. For example, the psychologist Barrie Irving conducted a study of police questioning for the Royal Commission on Criminal Procedure (see pp. 25–29). Psychologists at the MRC Applied Psychology Unit in Cambridge carried out studies for the Fraud Trials Committee chaired by Lord Roskill (see p. 54). The British Psychological Society may prepare evidence (as it did to the Butler Committee on the mentally abnormal offender in 1974) or statements on issues such as the use of the polygraph.

There are many other ways in which psychologists can and have contributed to policy questions. For instance, Ivan Brown of the MRC Applied Psychology Unit in Cambridge contributed a psychologist's perspective to questions about penalties for road traffic offences. He was invited to join a Council of Europe Working Group on Road Traffic Offences, whose task was to advise a committee of legal experts charged with the harmonization of penalties for traffic offences in member countries in Europe. Psychologists are currently working on developing methods of interviewing child victims of abuse in such a way as to provide acceptable evidence if videotaped interviews are made admissible in court. In the US, the American Psychological Association has made active efforts to influence judicial policy making by filing *amicus curiae* briefs in strategic legal cases.

HOW TO FIND THE RIGHT PSYCHOLOGIST

Most psychologists acting as experts come to do so through their employers or in the course of their normal employment as clinical or educational psychologists. Sometimes, however, a lawyer may seek a psychologist more directly. Private work is greatly on the increase. How can an appropriate psychologist be found? One method sometimes used is to circulate psychology departments in the universities or hospitals with a general enquiry. This may indeed find a psychologist, or several, but the procedure may trawl up all kinds of fish. Not all willing psychologists are also able! Telephoning the local university department is similarly a hazardous approach. It is obviously important to have some idea of the kind of psychologist who would be appropriate: the earlier parts of this chapter aim to help here.

Contact is often made by personal recommendation or through the psychologist's reputation in the appropriate field. Failing that, the professional body for psychologists in the UK – The British Psychological Society – is willing to try to help identify an appropriate person through its professional divisions and scientific sections. Enquiries can be made to The British Psychological Society, St Andrews House, 48 Princess Road East, Leicester LE1 7DR.

PSYCHOLOGISTS' DILEMMAS IN ACTING AS EXPERTS

Psychologists are often ambivalent about their roles (or others' roles) as experts. There are several reasons for this.

Who is the client?

A recurring dilemma for clinical psychologists is the question, 'Who is the client?' The question arises also for other psychologists who see clients in a clinical therapeutic setting. Professional ethics place responsibility on the psychologist to protect the interests of the patient. But when a psychologist has been engaged by a lawyer, he or she in a sense has two clients – the lawyer and the patient. Their interests may well conflict. What should the psychologist do if a suspect, for example, confesses to a crime but asks the psychologist not to tell anyone? As Lionel Haward points out, the setting in which a clinical interview takes place is very conducive to this kind of confidence. A suspect's expectation that his or her confidences will be respected may be increased by the assumption that the psychologist is a medical doctor. The kind of privacy expected of a usual medical consultation may be assumed to be operating. Conflict between the interests of the 'law' and those of a patient may also occur when forensic hypnosis is conducted (see Chapter 2). The psychologist may wish to protect the well-being of the hypnotic subject at the expense of obtaining useful information.

The ethics of taking sides

Another dilemma may arise when the psychologist realizes that there is more to be said for the 'other side', but he or she is not in a position to put this forward. Elizabeth Loftus (1986), for example, describes how the questions asked of an expert witness naturally tend to be selective and may omit to elicit relevant, but unfavourable facts. She raises the question 'Should the psychologist seek to act as advocate or as impartial educator?'

Loftus further illustrates this problem when discussing her involvement in the case involving bank logos, outlined above. Her results showed minimal confusion over the relevant logos. However, she points out that she could have designed a different study. She could have chosen to allow a much shorter time for studying the logos, or a much longer time between seeing the logos and trying to pick the one seen before. These procedures would undoubtedly have produced more errors and more confusion in general; and perhaps more confusion of the critical logos. Loftus points out that the ability to 'control' the outcome of special purpose experiments presents a dilemma for the researcher. The possibility of producing different answers in this way arises not from faults in the research design, but from imprecision in the question being posed. In this instance 'confusibility' of the logos was not precisely defined.

The pressure to give definite answers

As indicated in the Introduction, there are good reasons for psychologists to tread very carefully when applying the theories and research findings of psychology. Most psychological research is carried out in laboratory settings, and not designed to answer applied questions. The application of general principles to individual cases is especially hazardous. Generalizations based on research evidence may be true of the overwhelming majority of cases, but may happen not to apply to the case in question. Prediction of future behaviour and development is always to some degree uncertain, but legal cases have to be concluded one way or another, and a psychologist's sensitivities about the partial or provisional nature of psychological knowledge or the difficulty of firm prediction are not always welcome in this context.

One area that serves as an illustration of some of these problems is that of assessment of brain-injured patients for personal injury cases. This is an area where theory and psychological knowledge are constantly developing, and one where prediction can sometimes be extremely difficult.

Such assessments usually rely to a large extent on theories about the functions of different parts of the brain and how these develop. Damage to certain areas of the brain can produce classic clusters of difficulties, such as difficulties with language, or in learning and retaining new material, or in tasks that require work of the two sides of the brain to be co-ordinated. Bizarre disorders of memory sometimes become the subject of television documentaries, showing how otherwise 'normal' people suffer from problems of recognizing and remembering their surroundings, people they know, what has just happened, or everything else except what has just happened.

The activities of the brain are not divided absolutely and permanently between neatly specified areas. For example, people can perform normally with extraordinarily large areas of the brain damaged or missing. A child born with the whole of one cerebral hemisphere absent may show no symptoms. The ability of the unaffected hemisphere to take over the operation of an injured hemisphere diminishes rapidly after the age of a year, however. Sometimes spontaneous recovery of skills despite permanent brain damage indicates that the brain is carrying out the same task in a new way. The brain is now usually understood as a functional system. Each area has specific functions. Physiological and psychological observation show what these are. These specific functions in turn participate in a functional system, rather as the stomach participates in the digestive system.

The effects of an injury, especially an injury to a child, may not become apparent for some considerable time. This, of course, creates problems for compensation assessments. In one case, described by Charles Golden (1985), a child was injured at the age of three in a car accident. After the accident he had language problems, difficulties in drawing, and several other neurological deficits. Over the next two years he improved with therapy, and by the age of five, no deficits were found. His performance at school was consistent with his IQ and all seemed well. But at adolescence he suddenly began to appear less mature, and more impulsive than his peers. His grades at school began to fall off, and he got involved with 'bad company'. He was picked up for a robbery at the age of 16 in which he had taken all the risks and was easily caught. His condition grew worse as he failed to mature, and he ended up in a psychiatric hospital. There he was assessed by a neuropsychologist who found a pattern of deficits consistent with the injury he received at the age of three. However, when he was tested at the age of five, the later effects of the injury could not be picked up because the relevant skills were not expected of a normal five year old. All that might have been possible at that stage would have been to use knowledge of how the brain develops over time to state a probability of later problems.

Obviously the complexities of neuropsychological assessment are beyond the scope of this book (let alone my own expertise). The above is intended to illustrate how difficult it can be for a clinical psychologist to come up with a definite view on someone's capabilities or mental state and to predict their future behaviour. Problems of prediction are not peculiar to psychology of course. The above example comes very close to medicine where similar problems abound. In psychology, as in other fields, some cases are far more clear cut and their outcomes more predictable than others.

Where exactly we should draw the line and say that psychologists should refrain from acting as experts is a subject of growing debate amongst psychologists. As psychologists have begun to take on a more prominent role as experts, anxiety has arisen that psychology may be oversold, and that psychologists in offering apparently 'scientific' opinions, may exceed what psychology can actually deliver. Some psychologists, for example, have expressed serious reservations about the role of psychologists in cases involving children. In the US there has been disagreement over whether the state of psychological knowledge about eyewitness reliability is sufficiently developed to provide the basis of an expert opinion.

In practice it is not so often a question of psychologists enthusiastically offering opinions as being pressed to express one. Clinical and educational psychologists rarely seek out work in connection with the courts, and often perform this role somewhat reluctantly.

Who presents the psychology to the court?

As we have seen, psychologists sometimes contribute indirectly to expert evidence through a psychiatrist. This again creates a conflict between therapeutic and legal goals. The psychiatrist may well incorporate part of a psychologist's report in his or her report to the court. The psychologist's report forms part of the patient's file and may have been written for quite different, therapeutic purposes. But bits of it may then find their way, via the psychiatrist, to the court, even though this was never envisaged when the report was written. It is understandably a source of some worry to psychologists that their assessments and opinions can come to be presented second-hand in this way, sometimes without their knowledge. Responsible psychologists wish to control, and where appropriate limit the ways in which their skills, research findings and theories are used.

The use and misuse of psychologists in court

This leads us to another kind of difficulty for some groups of psychologists. All too often they feel that their evidence in court or in written reports is misunderstood, wasted or misused. Howard Parker (1987) describes how psychological evidence in juvenile courts (usually in written reports) is used in a cursory and selective way. It is quite likely to be ignored altogether by the magistrates. When it does affect their decisions this is likely to be in ways unintended by the psychologist. In juvenile court cases, the psychologist contributes not as an independent witness, so much as one among several professionals, and his or her contribution is orchestrated by others. It is not surprising that psychologists are often less than enthusiastic about involvement in legal cases. As psychologists gain more experience of acting as experts, and become familiar with the realities of the courts, they tend to become increasingly cynical about the role they are actually being asked to play.

Being cross-examined

The enthusiasm of some is dampened still further by the experience of appearing as a witness, and especially the experience of being cross-examined. As we have seen, psychological evidence is very likely to include the results of psychological tests. Sometimes cross-examination has taken the form of questioning about individual test items and details of testing procedures. This kind of questioning is usually irrelevant to an evaluation of the test results. As described above, the face-value relevance of individual test items is a very poor guide to the validity of a properly constructed and validated test. Any competent psychologist will also acknowledge that psychological tests do not yield absolute truths about people. The margins of possible error will have been studied during the development of the test, and allowed for in the psychologist's interpretation. Cross-examining lawyers, interested in demolishing the psychologist's evidence, have sometimes seized on individual test items or the possibility of error. Quite apart from the irrelevance of questioning a test item, this procedure threatens the confidentiality and validity of the test.

There is a growing recognition among professional bodies that psychologists need to be prepared during their training for work involving them as experts. This, combined with their increasing experience, should make them altogether tougher targets in the witness box.

In conclusion . . .

There are many different ways in which psychologists act as experts. The main groups involved are clinical and educational psychologists who give expert opinions on people's mental state and capabilities and draw the implications of their assessments for legal decisions about the individual concerned. Other groups include prison psychologists, occupational psychologists, and applied psychologists in many fields of psychology. It is essential to find an appropriate psychologist for any particular question. The methods used to provide the basis of expert opinions include clinical interviews and psychological testing, specially conducted experiments, and application of the more general literature to the particular case or issue.

In the great majority of cases where psychologists are involved no problems become apparent. But there are underlying tensions and pitfalls, and psychologists themselves are not always happy about taking on the role of 'expert' in legal cases. There are several reasons why they may feel this way. One is a reluctance to give a definite opinion when psychological prediction and diagnosis is always to some degree uncertain. A second is the ethical dilemmas that arise, especially when professional responsibility towards a patient conflicts with legal priorities. Psychologists engaged in trying to help or 'improve' the law venture into the sphere of societal values, and involvement in law, whether in the role of expert or in policy formation, brings ethical responsibilities. Lastly, psychologists are increasingly dismayed at their experiences of an adversarial system, and disillusioned about their role and purpose when their advice is permitted (or sought) by lawyers. Sometimes their role may turn out to be little more than token and what they have to say may in the end have little to do with the decisions that get taken. In some cases, such as those concerning children, lawyers who find the decisions they have to make impossibly difficult, may be only too happy to pass the buck to an 'expert'. Judge Bazelon warned a meeting of correctional psychologists in the US:

Before you respond with enthusiasm to our plea for help, you must ask yourselves whether your help is really needed, or whether you are merely engaged as magicians to perform an intriguing side-show so that the spectators will not notice the crisis in the center ring. In considering our motives for offering you a role, I think you would do well to consider how much less expensive it is to hire a thousand psychologists than to make even a minuscule change in the social and economic structure. (Tapp and Levine, 1977)

References

Clapham, Judge B. (1981) Introducing psychological evidence in the courts: Impediments and opportunities. In S.M.A. Lloyd-Bostock (ed.) *Psychology in Legal Contexts: Applications and Limitations*. London: Macmillan.

Golden, C.J. (1985) Forensic neuropsychology: Introduction and overview. In C.J. Golden and M.A. Strider (ed.) *Forensic Neuropsychology*. New York: Plenum.

*Haward, L.R.C. (1981) *Forensic Psychology*. London: Batsford.

Loftus, E.F. (1986) Experimental psychologist as advocate or impartial educator? *Law and Human Behaviour*, 10, 1/2 (Special Issue on 'The Ethics of Expert Testimony') 63–78.

Parker, H. (1987) The use of reports in juvenile and magistrates' courts. In G. Gudjonsson and J. Drinkwater (ed.) *Psychological Evidence in Court*. Leicester: Division of Criminological and Legal Psychology of The British Psychological Society.

Sutton, A. and Moss, G. (1984) Towards a forensic child psychology. In S.M.A. Lloyd-Bostock (ed.) *Children and the Law*. Oxford: Centre for Socio-Legal Studies.

Tapp, J.L. and Levine, F.J. (1977) Reflections and redirections. In J.L. Tapp and F.J. Levine (ed.) *Law, Justice and the Individual in Society*. New York: Holt, Rinehart & Winston.

Further reading

Publications marked with an asterisk (*) above.

Gudjonsson, G. and Drinkwater, J. (ed.) (1987) *Psychological Evidence in Court*. Leicester: Division of Criminological and Legal Psychology of The British Psychological Society.

McLoskey, M., Egeth, H. and McKenna, J. (1986) *The Ethics of Expert Testimony, Law and Human Behaviour*, 10, 1/2 (Special Issue).

Chapter 8

A Broader View of Psychology's Usefulness

Throughout the book I have emphasized that psychology can be applied much more confidently to some questions than others. At some points I indicated that psychology's application to the particular question under discussion was tentative or speculative; at others I said it was much more definite. So when can psychological research findings be safely applied to practical legal questions? When should psychological 'knowledge' be preferred to legal decision makers' own common sense?

The confidence with which psychology can be applied depends partly on what sort of research has been done and partly on the proposed use of the findings. Where the research itself is concerned, a central problem is that of generalizing from the laboratory to actual legal settings.

THE LABORATORY AND THE 'REAL WORLD'

I have referred to a great many psychology experiments in the course of this book. Laboratory experiments have powerful advantages as a research method, and are by far the method most frequently chosen by psychologists. An experiment allows the researcher to disentangle alternative possibilities and examine them systematically. But the precision and flexibility of the laboratory experiment is bought at a price. We do not know whether results obtained in an artificially controlled setting hold true also of 'real life'.

Laboratory studies of jury decision making illustrate well the advantages and drawbacks of a laboratory experiment for studying legal processes. Simulations of jury trials in the laboratory allow psychologists to tackle all sorts of questions that could not be looked at systematically in any other way. For example, one study described in Chapter 3 examined the effects on juries of an instruction to ignore information about insurance in a damages case. Such a question can best be answered by comparing three alternatives: 1) what happens with such an instruction; 2) what happens without it; and 3) what happens without the information at all. This is exactly what a laboratory experiment can be designed to do. An experiment involves carefully comparing what happens under at least two different sets of conditions. Where psychology experiments are concerned this means exposing people (or sometimes animals) to one of two or more different experiences, and measuring any differences in their behaviour: in the case of the jury experiment, any differences in the juries' decisions. But simulations of jury trials in the laboratory inevitably differ in important ways from actual courtroom settings – not least in that the 'verdict' of a mock jury does not carry important consequences for a real defendant. The experiment may have a neat internal logic. But do the results generalize to actual jurors in a real case?

Just occasionally it proves possible to combine the advantages of an experiment with those of 'real world' research. A rare example is Ian Berg's research with his colleagues in Leeds, mentioned in Chapter 5. The research involved the court randomly allocating school truants to different treatments. The study shows how random allocation – an essential part of a psychology experiment – makes interpretation of research results much more definite. Truancy cases often arose where the magistrates felt there was no good reason to favour either adjournment of the case or a supervision order. In such cases the magistrates used a random allocation procedure to decide what to do. (They lifted the next in a series of sticky labels and used whichever treatment was specified underneath.) The results were clear. Adjournment was a far more effective means of making children attend school.

Without the random allocation procedure the explanation could have been that different sorts of children were being assigned to the two treatments. Factors such as age, intelligence and home background might relate to willingness to return to school. The purpose of random allocation was to ensure that each treatment group had an equal chance of having willing children in it. The researchers were therefore in a strong position to conclude that the different outcomes were due to the different treatments.

For obvious reasons, Berg's research is something of a special case. It is not usually possible to introduce random allocation into real legal proceedings. Moreover, a researcher often wants to compare what happens under various conditions that do not conveniently occur naturally. Usually, conducting an experiment means creating experimental conditions in the laboratory.

How, then, are we ever to bridge the gap and generalize from the results of laboratory experiments to actual legal settings and legal processes? Should psychologists select other methods when they want to be able to apply their results to a practical, 'real life' problem?

WHEN CAN PSYCHOLOGY BE APPLIED TO 'REAL LIFE'?

There are three main characteristics of research that increase our confidence that its findings apply to practical, 'real life' questions. First and foremost we can be more confident in applying research that is carried out in realistic or natural settings. Secondly, we can be more confident if a substantial number of studies all point to the same conclusion. Thirdly, we can be more confident when well-established psychological theory accounts for the findings. Conversely generalizations from research findings are on less certain ground when these three features of research are absent. (Many volumes have been written on research design and methodology. I am not concerned here with basic research competence but with the generalizability of competent research to legal contexts.)

1. Making research realistic

If experiments are used to study practical questions, they need to be as realistic as possible. For example, simulated studies of juries need to ensure that the mock jurors used are similar to actual jurors and not simply a group of students. The experiment on the effects of instructions to ignore information drew its mock jurors from people actually summoned to serve as jurors. Researchers interested in eyewitness reliability have devised some elaborate *field experiments*. The experience to which the people in these experiments are exposed is made as realistic as possible, by having them witness what they believe is a genuine dramatic incident of some kind. Experiments using live events do sometimes produce different results from less realistic studies using videotape or slides, showing how dangerous it is to generalize from less realistic settings to real cases.

One problem here is the ethics of deceiving and experimenting on people without their consent. People are not always pleased to learn that an incident they have become involved in was a psychology experiment. The research by Gail Goodman described in Chapter 5 ingeniously overcame the ethical problems that can arise when a researcher needs to subject people to realistic experiences. Goodman was interested in children's memories for incidents involving sexual abuse. As a proxy for the obvious impossibilities of simulating such an event, she studied children's memory for a visit to an inoculation clinic – an unpleasant event involving coerced physical contact with a stranger.

Sometimes experiments are simply not a feasible or appropriate way of studying a practical question, and another method should be chosen. Psychology is a discipline that tackles all sorts of different questions. Some (such as questions about the physiology of perception) lend themselves much more readily to an experimental approach than others (the behaviour of football crowds for example).

The main alternative to an experiment is a *correlational study*, examining how two or more factors interrelate. This method usually produces more ambiguous results than an experiment, but it has the great advantage that it can be used to study much more natural settings. For example, if Berg and his team had not been able to obtain co-operation in randomly allocating truants, they might have simply related the treatments chosen in a large sample of cases to their outcome. This would certainly have given an indication of how the two treatments compared. As we have seen, the random allocation procedure was designed to rule out the possibility of systematic differences between the groups of cases being treated in each way. Without that procedure, many ambiguities would have remained. But it is difficult to see how the comparative effectiveness of the two procedures could ever meaningfully be studied in a laboratory.

Often an approach using several different methods in combination is appropriate for studying practical questions. I described a good example in Chapter 3. The programme of research in the US on language in the courtroom led by William O'Barr began with an extended period of observation and recording of actual court proceedings. This stage then provided the basis for a series of experiments. The laboratory research was thus firmly rooted in actual examples of courtroom speech. Other possible methods that lend themselves to 'real life' settings are surveys, interviews and participant observation, where the researcher does not merely observe but takes part in the process being studied.

Sometimes the sequence is reversed. Rather than starting with a stage of observation, the results of experimental work are checked in a 'real life' setting. Thus, John Yuille and Judith Cutshall took advantage of a real crime to see how far findings from experimental eyewitness research were borne out (see Chapter 1). Their study was the first of its kind. Twenty-one witnesses to an actual shooting were interviewed by the police, and 13 of them took part in later interviews for the research project. The researchers analysed in detail both the police interviews and their own later interviews. They found a higher level of accuracy than previous eyewitness research might have led them to expect, and suggest the unexpected accuracy was due to the striking and unique character of the event, beyond anything that could ethically be staged for research purposes. Yuille and Cutshall's study tested how far ideas from previous research stand up in the context of a real crime. It also raised new questions – for example, about memory for colour – that could be taken back to the laboratory and investigated experimentally.

The main way in which confidence in the applicability of research is increased therefore, is by studying realistic or natural events. When realistic or natural experiments are not feasible, alternative methods, or a combination of methods, are called for.

2. The amount of research evidence

I have already emphasized that one study on its own very rarely provides the basis for practical conclusions. If several studies in different contexts using different methods and paradigms point to the same conclusion we can be much more confident. A single result leaves too many alternative possibilities open.

Patrick Rabbitt (1981) gives a good example. He draws on his own experiments on the recall of old people to show just how tempting it is to leap to a mistaken practical conclusion from too few experimental results. In an experiment designed to compare memory efficiency in young and elderly people, he showed his subjects 300 words, one at a time. As each word was shown they had to say whether or not it was one they had seen before in the list. Two types of error were counted: failure to recognize a word previously seen, and false identification of a word which had not in fact been previously seen. The results showed that the elderly made more errors than the young, but that almost none of these were false identifications.

This result might tempt one to make the generalization that when elderly people fail to recall a particular event, they are less likely to confabulate than young people. However, further experiments showed that when the task was changed and the subjects were required to *recall* words, rather than recognize them, the older subjects recalled fewer words than the younger, but also 'recalled' many words which had not been presented to them. Any generalization as to whether the old people were more or less prone to confabulate based on the first experiment would clearly have been unreliable. Further experiments showed that even the more detailed assertion that old people confabulate in recall but not in recognition would also have been mistaken.

Plentiful evidence from a variety of sources can partially compensate for weaknesses of individual pieces of research. For example, studies of children's reactions to divorce often look only at children whose parents *have* divorced. There is no comparison group of children whose parents have not divorced (and clearly there is no question of randomly allocating children to divorce and no divorce). The Wallerstein and Kelly research described in Chapter 5 studied families who had voluntarily come for counselling at the time of divorce. If we had only their research to go on, we would not know to what extent many of the findings were attributable to the divorce, and to what extent they simply described patterns of behaviour typical of children in a variety of family contexts. Nor would we know how far they described only the particular type of family who made up the rather selective sample. But the research can be taken together with other studies of children of divorce, and a much greater number of other studies of children in various family situations. Uncertainties still remain, but they are much reduced by the fact that certain central findings are consistent with other sources of evidence.

In the book I have sometimes generalized from research in contexts quite different from those I was discussing on the basis that findings were consistent across several contexts. When discussing sentencing in Chapter 4, I drew on theory about the way decision making becomes more automatic with experience. That theory was developed through research in several settings where decisions with important parallels with sentencing are taken, such as medical diagnosis. Similarly, in Chapter 3 on persuasion in the courtroom, I suggested some ways in which research in other settings on the persuasiveness of messages might apply to courtroom communications. As I pointed out at the time, these remain speculative suggestions until the relevant research is done in the context in question.

3. Theory

However high the pile of research findings, it can be impossible to draw useful general implications from them without a well-established theoretical framework. It is not enough to discover that something occurs, we need to have a psychological understanding of *why* it occurs. To use Berg's research again as an example, the research team showed clearly that adjournment worked better with truants than supervision. But unless we have an understanding of why it worked better, we cannot use the findings beyond their immediate context. We have no basis for judging whether the crucial factors are present in other courts, or for other offences.

Collecting data in further contexts can help, but unless theory develops, more data tend to complicate matters rather than make sense of them. This is what happened to early research in the area of eyewitness reliability. Studies of eyewitness reliability around the beginning of the twentieth century produced a mass of intriguing findings. But it was impossible to make coherent sense of them until advances were made in *theories* of memory. The practical implications of the research remained elusive for many years. Nowadays, theory in the areas of perception and memory in itself suggests new ways of looking at eyewitness reliability. In Chapter 4 I criticized much of the existing research on sentencing as simply relating a range of factors to the sentence awarded in a somewhat atheoretical way, rather as the early eyewitness researchers did.

Of course, theories can and do turn out to be wrong. The better established the theory, the safer are generalizations based on research that uses it. Often a well-established theory will seem to be relevant to a legal question, or aspect of legal processes, but research to test its applicability has not been done. I referred above to my own extension of theories of decision making to sentencing. As I stressed then, application of theory in a new and different context remains speculative until the relevant research is done. It can be tempting to generalize too far or too firmly from plausible psychological theories.

Up to a point, common sense can give confidence in research in the same way as sound theory does. If results ring true and make sense to the people involved, that is a hopeful sign. Indeed, some research methods give primary importance to the common-sense theories about what they are doing held by participants in the process being studied. However, some of psychology's most important findings seem strange at first, or are hard to accept because they threaten people's beliefs. I suggested in previous chapters that common-sense ideas about such things as how memory works, why people confess, and what factors influence decisions, can be misleading.

Are the findings significant?

Research findings can be highly significant from an academic point of view, but of no *practical* significance at all. Whether a research hypothesis is considered to be supported or rejected depends on the notion of *statistical* significance. The statistical significance of a result is an estimate of how often such a result might come up purely by chance. A 'significance level' of less than .001 means that there is a less than one in a thousand probability that this is a chance result. Usually a .01 (one in a hundred) level is accepted as a statistically significant result.

Statistical significance tells us how sure we can be that an effect exists. It does not tell us how large the effect is. Statistical significance is also related to the amount of variation in the data and to the size of the sample. In a large enough sample, a very small effect indeed can be highly significant. It is easy, and a mistake, to confuse statistical significance with practical significance. For instance suppose a research paper reported that children from broken homes were found to be 'significantly' more likely to show symptoms of anxiety than other children. This could still mean that most children (of divorce or otherwise) showed no symptoms at all; or the difference could be slight but reach statistical significance over a large sample.

To be of practical significance a research finding needs to be not just reliable but also *relevant* to a practical problem and its effect large enough to be worth considering as the basis for practical action.

Is it relevant to a practical problem?

It is risky to draw practical implications from research that was not designed to answer practical questions. At times in the book I have suggested that psychologists and lawyers alike need to pay more attention to the question of defining just what are the 'problems' that psychology might help to solve. Psychologists who have turned their research interests to law have relied to a great extent on their common-sense ideas about legal processes. As a result some have tended to place the courts too much at the centre of the stage, and to proceed as if the purpose of such procedures as trials, identification parades, and interviews with witnesses and suspects were straightforward and unambiguous.

Much of the early research effort in law and psychology was rooted primarily in questions of psychological rather than legal interest. Large numbers of early jury studies, for example, were essentially studies in small group decision making conducted by psychologists who wished to make their research more socially relevant. One psychologist, Neil Vidmar, pointed out in 1979 that in jury simulations psychologists had been using situations that simply do not arise in real cases. For example, they had confused the procedures in criminal trials with civil trials. One simulation involved the jury hearing a discussion about the admissibility of evidence that would not be held in their presence in a real trial.

As the field of psychology and law develops, psychologists researching legal topics are now more often qualified in both law and psychology, and have more experience of the realities of legal processes than in the past. Even so, it is still important to ask what exactly are the research questions and where do they come from.

Useful for what purpose?

So far I have indicated the main questions to be asked in deciding whether research (assuming it is competently conducted) can safely be applied in legal contexts:

* What questions was the research designed to answer?
* How realistic was the research setting?
* What method (or combination of methods) was used?
* How much evidence is there from different sources pointing to the same conclusion?
* Is there well-established theory to account for the findings?
* How large and how reliable are the effects that have been found?

The answers one would need before deciding whether psychology research can be applied will depend on what exactly it is to be applied to. The considerations listed above weigh differently in individual cases, applications to legal skills, policy applications and more general uses of psychology to provide insights into legal processes.

A further consideration in clinical approaches to individual cases, and also in legal skills training, is: Does it work? From the practical point of view the research and theory behind a psychologist's advice and recommendations may be less important than its consequences. Similarly, the proof of training techniques is their effectiveness.

I have stressed throughout the book that direct applications in specific cases need to be made with more caution than more general applications to policy. The chances of getting things right need to be high. In Chapter 1, for example, I concluded that eyewitness research has clear implications for policy on such matters as police interviewing and identification procedures, but that the evaluation of a specific piece of evidence in a particular case is much less certain. As described in the last chapter, a specially designed study or clinical work is usually needed before psychology can be on sufficiently sure grounds to be applied to an individual case.

However, psychologists can sometimes make a legitimate contribution in a particular case even when it is not possible to give a clear and definite statement or answer to a specific question. The law constantly deals with probabilities. How much certainty it is appropriate to demand depends on the particular case. In the previous chapter I described a case of brain injury to a child to illustrate how uncertain long-term prediction can be. Yet even a small probability of later problems developing can be compensated and is therefore relevant to a case for compensation. A British court will award damages proportionately to the probability. If there is a 10 per cent chance of osteoarthritis eventually developing as a result of an injury, then the victim should be awarded 10 per cent of damages he or she would get if the disease were certain to develop.

In criminal cases, even if it is not possible to give a definite evaluation of the reliability of certain evidence, the probability of an error may still be enough to introduce 'reasonable doubt'. For example, in a case that relies on identification evidence, factors may accumulate to make the identification evidence too unreliable. Such a case was highlighted by the British television programme *Rough Justice* in October 1987. A man had been convicted of taking part in a robbery on the basis of identification evidence. There were many question marks over the reliability of the evidence. It was obtained after some delay from witnesses who had been questioned and shown photographs in the meantime. Only two out of over twenty possible eyewitnesses picked the suspect from an identification parade, and then only after the parade was repeated. What is more, the man had a particularly memorable appearance. He was very tall, had red hair, and a broken, crooked nose. It seemed improbable that he had been at the places in question and passed unnoticed by so many potential witnesses. In these circumstances, a psychologist is able to say that, however sincere and honest the witnesses, the chances that the identification evidence is mistaken are unacceptably high.

As well as the probability of being right, a crucial aspect of using psychology in individual cases is the cost of getting things *wrong* and what the alternatives are. Compare, for example, the decision to remove a young child from its family with the decision to try a programme of behaviour therapy with a car thief. Both are decisions likely to involve a psychologist. Where the car thief is concerned the psychologist could rightly take into account that little is likely to be lost by trying, and much may be gained. Far more is at stake in the decision about the child. The wrong decision either way carries high costs.

Where the present state of psychology does not permit practical inferences to be drawn in relation to a specific legal case or policy issue, or an aspect of legal skills, psychology can still often make a contribution of a less obvious kind. In the book I have discussed several areas where psychology's message is ambivalent or provisional. Rather than regard them as areas where psychology has not yet succeeded in being useful, I have taken a broader view of the ways in which lawyers may find psychology useful – for example in bringing a different perspective to the functioning of juries, to why people confess, or to sentencing; or in showing that, while we do not yet know the best answer, we can say that some custody arrangements have no sound psychological basis. Psychology can offer important insights, throw doubt on established beliefs, or clarify the dimensions of a problem without necessarily prescribing the solution.

This broader view of psychology's usefulness to lawyers underlies much of what I have written in the book – on witnesses, the courtroom, and children in particular. My aim in these chapters was not so much to come up with specific practical recommendations (though some are possible) but rather to show how the various processes involved look from a psychological perspective. Psychology often cannot provide a clear 'scientific' solution to a practical legal problem. But it can very often make other, less ambitious and more legitimate contributions to law in practice.

References

Rabbitt, P.M.A. (1981) Applying human experimental psychology to legal questions about evidence. In S.M.A. Lloyd-Bostock (ed.) *Psychology in Legal Contexts: Applications and Limitations.* London: Macmillan.

Vidmar, N. (1979) The other issues in jury simulation research: A commentary with particular reference to defendant character studies. *Law and Human Behaviour 3, 1/2,* (Special Issue on 'Simulation Research and the Law'), 95–106.

Author Index

Page numbers in *italics* indicate a reference entry

ALEXANDER, J.R. *106*
Allen, H. 76, 77, 78, 79, *81*
Argyle, M.A. 109, *135*
Ashworth, A. 69, *81*
Avetissian, I. 22

BALDWIN, J. 53, *60*
Barlett, J. *34*
Bazelon, Judge *156*
Benson Report 108, 109, *135*
Berg, I. 104, *106*, 159, *163*
Binder, D.A. 134, *135*
Blumberg, A. 75, *82*
Bowlby, J. 95
Brandon, R. 26, *35*
Bray, R.M. 58, *60*
Brittan, Y. *136*
Broadbent, D.E. 66, 67, *81*
Brown, I. 150
Burgoyne, J. *107*
Burns, T.E. 7, 22

CHARROW, R. 55, *60*, *129*
Charrow, V. 55, 60, *129*
Clapham, Judge B. *157*
Clifford, B.R. 22, 23, *36*
Conley, J. 38
Cooke, Judge R.K. 70, *81*
Corfield, P. *136*
Coutts, J.A. 56, *60*
Cutshall, J.L. 10, 22, 161, 162

DAVIES, C. 26, *35*
Davies, G.M. 11, 12, 22, 88, *106*, *107*

Dell, S. 78, 79, *81*
Dent, H.R. 16, 22
Devine, P.G. 5, 14, 22
Devlin, Lord 3, 14, 22
Drinkwater, J. *107*, *157*

EBBESEN, E. 66, 76, *81*
Eekelaar, J. 97, *106*
Egeth, H. *157*
Ellis, H.D. 22
England, P. *106*
Evans, D.R. *134*
Ewart, B. 74, *81*

FARRINGTON, D.P. 22, *106*, *136*
Fenn, P. *136*
Firstenberg, I. 22
Fisher, Sir H. 24, *35*
Fisher, R. 22, 109, 123, *135*
Fitzmaurice, C. 67, 71, 72, *81*
Flin, R. 88, *106*
Frank, J. 63, *81*
Freud, A. 95, *106*

GALE, A. 31, *36*
Geiselman, R.E. 11, 20, 22
Genders, E. *81*
Genn, H. 121, 122, 123, 124, *135*
Gibson, H.B. 17, 20, 22
Giller, H. 99, 102, 104, *107*
Golden, C.J. 153, *157*
Goldstein, J. 95, *106*
Goodman, G. 85, 89, *106*, 160
Gudjonsson, G.H. 28, 32, 35, *36*, *157*

HANS, V. 49, 50, 51, 52, 53, *60*
Harris, D. 121, 125, *135*
Hastie, R. 46, 58, *60*
Haward, L.R.C. 17, 19, 20, *22*, 143, 144, 148, 149, 151, *157*
Hawkins, K.O.H. *22*, 76, *81*, *106*, *136*
Hearn, M.T. *135*
Henderson, R.W. *106*
Hetherington, M. 91, *106*
Hilgendorf, E.L. 16, *22*, 26, 27, 28, *36*
Hogarth, J. 74, 75, *81*
Homel, R. 63, 68, *82*
Hullin, R. *106*
Hutton, L.A. *22*

ILFIELD, F.W. 94, *106*
Ilfield, M.Z. *106*
Inbau, F.E. 24, 25, 27, *36*
Ingleby, R. 126
Irving, B.L. 16, *22*, 25, 26, 27, 28, *36*
Ivey, A.E. *135*

JONES, D.P.H. *106*

KALVEN, H. 53, 57, *60*
Kelly, J.B. 90, 92, 93, 94, 97, 98, *106*, *107*, 163
Kerr, N.L. 58, *60*
Konecni, V. 66, 76, *81*

LAWRENCE, J. 63, 68, *82*
Levine, F.J. 157, *157*
Lind, A. 38, *60*
Lloyd-Bostock, S.M.A. *22*, *23*, *36*, 71, *81*, *82*, *106*, *107*, 125, *136*, *157*, *168*
Loftus, E.F. 7, 8, 9, *22*, *23*, 149, 152, *157*
Loftus, G.R. *22*
Lovegrove, A. 75, *82*
Lykken, D.T. 31, 32, 33, 34, *36*

MCCONVILLE, M. 53, *60*
McGuire, R. 106
McKenna, J. *157*
Maclean, M. 96, 97, *106*, *107*, *136*
McLoskey, M. *157*
Malpass, R.S. 14, 16, *22*
Mansfield, G. *81*
Mason, R. *106*
Messo, J. *22*
Milgram, S. 27, 28, *36*
Mitchell, A. 91, *106*
Morris, N. *22*
Moss, G. 144, 145, *157*

NATIONAL CONSUMER COUNCIL 127, 130, 131, 135, *136*
Nisbett, R. 64, 65, *82*

O'BARR, W.M. 38, 40, 41, 42, 43, 49, *60*, 161
Ormrod, R. *107*
Orne, M.T. 18, 19, *22*

PALMER, J.C. 9, *22*
Parker, H. 155, *157*
Payne, J.W. 68, *82*
Pearson, J. 93
Pease, K. 67, 71, 72, *81*
Peay, J. *81*
Pennington, D.C. 71, 74, *81*, *82*
Pennington, N. 58, *60*
Penrod, S. 58, *60*
Petrie, C. 105, *106*
Player, E. *81*
Port, L.K. *106*
Potas, I. *82*
Prado-Estrada, L. *106*
Price, S.L. 34, *135*
Prosk, A. *22*
Pyle, E.A. *106*

RABBITT, P.M. 162, *168*
Redmount, R.S. 134, *136*
Reid, J.E. 24, 25, 27, *36*
Richards, M. 95, 96, 98, 99, *106*, *107*
Roskill, Lord P.C. 47, 54, *60*, 150
Ross, L. 65, *82*
Rudy, L. *106*
Rutter, M. 99, 102, 104, *107*

SAKS, M.J. 46, *60*
Schaffer, T.L. 134, *135*
Scott, D.M.M. 128, *136*
Shapland, J. 76, *82*
Shepherd, J.W. 14, *22*
Sherr, A. 108, 110, 111, 112, 114, 115, 118, 119, 135, *136*
Sim, R.S. 128, *136*
Smith, A. 75, *82*
Solnit, 95, *106*
Sommer, R. 5, *22*
Spencer, J. 86, *107*
Stephenson, G.M. 16, *22*
Strider, M.A. *157*
Sullivan, S. *22*
Sutton, A. 144, 145, *157*

TAPP, J.L. 157, *157*
Thibaut, J. 46, *60*
Thoeness, N. 93
Thomas, D. 64, *82*

Tonry, M. 22
Trankell, A. 6, 7, 22
Twining, W. 4, 23

UHLEMANN, M.R. 135
Ury, W. 109, 123, 135

VIDMAR, N. 49, 50, 51, 52, 53, 60, 165, 168

WADSWORTH, M. 96, 107
Walker, L. 46, 60
Wallerstein, J. 90, 92, 93, 94, 107, 163

Wallsten, T.S. 82
Weiner, B. 73, 82
Weitzman, L. 93, 94, 107
Wells, G.L. 23
Wickens, C.D. 62, 82
Williams, G. 52
Williams, G.R. 120, 122, 123, 136
Wilson, T. 64, 82

YUILLE, J.C. 10, 23, 161, 162

ZEISEL, H. 53, 57, 60

Subject Index

AMERICAN PSYCHOLOGICAL ASSOCIATION 150
American Telephone and Telegraph Company 50, 51
anatomically correct dolls 88, 89
Applied Psychology Unit, Cambridge 54, 139, 150

BRITISH PSYCHOLOGICAL SOCIETY, The 35, 84, 137, 150, 151
Broadmoor hospital 79
Butler Committee 150

CENTRE FOR SOCIO-LEGAL STUDIES, Oxford 121, 122, 126, 139
childhood 83–84, 106
Criminal Investigation Department 25, 26, 28
clinical psychologists 137, 138, 139, 144, 149, 151, 154, 156
compensation cases 4, 55–56, 121–122, 123, 124–126, 128, 129, 137, 144, 145, 148–149, 167
comprehensibility
  of advice to clients 117–118
  of documents 1, 109, 127–133, 135
  of evidence in court 49, 54
  of juror instructions 54–57
  see also information
Confait, Maxwell 25, 28, 140
confession 1, 24–30
  admitted as evidence 24, 29
  and the polygraph 33–34, 35
  by suspects with mental handicaps 25, 29
  expert evidence on 142
  false 24, 25, 26, 29, 34
  psychology of 26–30
  see also suggestibility

DAVIS, George 3
decision making
  automatic 62–64
  by judges and magistrates 61–81
  decision to confess 26–28
  errors in 67–68
  reasons given for 64–66
  see also juries; sentencing
delinquency 99–105
diminished responsibility 78
Division of Criminological and Legal Psychology 84
divorce counselling 99, 163
divorce, economic effects 97, 99
divorce, effects on children 1, 90–99, 101, 103, 163
  relationship with absent parent 92–94, 98, 99
divorce negotiation 94, 126
Dougherty, Luke 3
drafting see comprehensibility

EDUCATIONAL PSYCHOLOGISTS 38–39, 137, 144, 151, 156
ethical issues
  in conducting research 7, 160–161, 162
  in the use of the polygraph 35
  in role of expert 2, 151–152, 154, 156
experimental studies
  advantages of 158–159
  as basis for expert evidence 148–149, 156

expert evidence 1, 2, 21, 90, 137–157

FACIAL RECOGNITION, psychology of 12–14
Federal Bureau of Investigation 17
field experiments *see* staged events
Fretwell, David 12, 13

GENERALIZING FROM RESEARCH FINDINGS 2, 152–154, 158–168
Guildford Four 25

HAIN, Peter 3, 4
Hanratty, James 3, 14
Hillside Strangler 21, 50
Homicide Act 1957 79
Hutcheson, Judge 63
hypnosis 17–21
  expert evidence based on 142, 144

IDENTIFICATION PARADES 10, 14–16, 165, 167
Identikit 10, 11–12
Ince, George 3, 10
information
  available to sentencers 62, 69–70, 75–78, 79–80
  eliciting from clients 112–117
  presentation of in court 45–47, 163
interrogation, police 24–30, 33–35, 150
interviewing skills 1, 2, 108, 109–119
  see also questioning techniques

JOINT CUSTODY 93–94
juries 1, 2, 37, 44, 45, 47–60, 158–159, 165
  competence 52–57
  'death qualified' 49–50
  jury selection 50–52
  prejudice 48–50
  see also comprehensibility
juvenile courts 100, 104–105, 138, 155

LANGUAGE IN COURT 2, 38–43, 161
  see also comprehensibility
Lattimore 25, 28
lie detection 30–35, 140
  polygraph techniques 30–32, 144, 150
  see also confession
'List D' schools 105

MCI COMMUNICATION CORPORATION 50, 51
Meeham, Patrick 3
memory, psychology of 4–10

expectations and memory 4, 5–6
  children's 87–88, 160–161
  old peoples' 162–163
  'pseudo-memories' 18
  stress and memory 6–8
  see also suggestibility
mental abnormality 1, 29, 76–79, 92, 138, 140–141, 142–145, 150, 153–154
Mental Health Act 1983 78
Miranda v. *Arizona* 24
mistaken identity 3, 4

NEGOTIATING 1, 2, 47, 108, 109, 118–127, 113–135
  involvement of psychologists in 143
neuropsychology 140, 146, 153–154
non-verbal communication 109, 112–116, 140

OBSCENE PUBLICATIONS ACT 1959 141
occupational psychologists 139, 145, 154, 156

PENRY, Jacques 11
perception 4, 5–8, 14
personal injury *see* compensation
Photofit 10, 11–12
Police and Criminal Evidence Act 1984 25, 26, 28
Powers of the Criminal Courts Act 1973 78
prison psychologists 139, 156
prosopagnosia 14
psychiatric reports 76–78, 79–80, 154
psychiatrists 140–141, 154, 155
psychoanalytic thinking 95–96
psychological prediction, uncertainty of 152–154, 156, 167
psychological tests 145–148, 155–156

QUESTIONING TECHNIQUES, witnesses 1, 10–14, 140
  the cognitive interview 11, 20
  with children 88–90, 150
  see also suggestibility; interviewing skills; interrogation

REILLY, Peter 34
Road Research Laboratory, Berks. 139
Royal Commission on Criminal Procedure 26, 150

SENTENCING 1, 2, 61–81, 163, 164
  attribution theory 73–74
  disparity 69, 70

need for feedback 69–70, 81
of juveniles 104–105, 159
the arithmetic of 71–73
see also decision making
speech style 38–43, 49
Stafford, Jane 53
staged events 4, 7–8, 160–161
statistical significance 164–165
suggestibility
  and hypnosis 18–21
  and leading questions 9–10
  and photographs of suspects 10, 21
  interrogation 28–30, 140, 143
  of children 88–89, 143

TRUANCY 104, 159, 163–164
Twelve Angry Men 58

UNSWORN EVIDENCE OF CHILDREN 86–87

VIDEO-LINK SYSTEM 86
videotapes in court 46, 86, 90, 150
Virag, Lazlo 3

WEAPON FOCUS 8
witnesses, accuracy of 1, 2, 3–23,
  86–89, 140, 161–162
  expert evidence on 2, 21, 141, 150,
  154, 166, 167
  see also memory; questioning
  techniques; identification parades
witnesses, children as 84–89
  emotional disturbance among 1,
  84–86
  see also suggestibility
witnesses, credibility of 43–45, 49, 59
  see also speech style